Short Walks on

Long Island

by RODNEY *and* PRISCILLA ALBRIGHT

OLD CHESTER ROAD
CHESTER, CONNECTICUT 06412

First Printing, April, 1974
Second Printing, June, 1974
Third Printing, May, 1975
Fourth Printing, May, 1976

We walk to get fresh air, exercise, and to learn more about the world in which we live. In two of these respects Long Island offers unique opportunities.

It has a steadier flow of air than other places along the Atlantic coast and is, for this reason, fresh. The ocean off-shore tempers Long Island winters and makes the climate mild. From the first of July till early October, the water temperatures vary from 63° to 66°, while the air seldom, if ever, reaches 90°. To illustrate the important influence of the ocean in the moderation of its climate, the air in winter only occasionally will go as low as zero, while the water is never below 35°, providing a longer growing season here than other places of the same latitude. So the air is good country air.

And, as for physical features, Long Island has all three of the basic environments which ecologists study—salt water, fresh water, and terrestrial—intermingled with the complex presence of man, so walking here provides lots to see and ponder in regard to the fragile relationships of life.

Finally, the amount of exercise is directly related to your effort. Since walking here is not difficult, time regulates this.

The walks in this book do not include all possibilities. They are ones we've taken, many of them, many times, and recommend. Each is short, never strenuous, but can easily be extended and made more so if you wish.

We've grouped the walks into categories with physical similarities, and which fall together, to allow us the liberty to try to suggest a few possible things to look for. You'll find, as we have, most of these walks can be taken again and again, and always, we believe, with new interest.

Walking on Long Island

Walking on Long Island takes you into bracing air, clears your mind, sharpens your senses. It's refreshing. You don't have to scramble over rocks, follow blazes, have any fear of getting lost, or worry about equipment. You can start off pretty much as you are and come back refueled. We've been walking on Long Island, mostly on weekends, for years now and we enthusiastically recommend it. Here are some suggestions:

Don't try to get a group together. Much of this land is owned privately and the fewer of you the less nuisance. Space is limited so parking, particularly in summer months, is often restricted to village permit holders. An effort is made, as it should be, to limit the numbers of persons using the land, so act like a guest. You will take a train, or find a place to park, and a couple on foot is seldom challenged when they mind their own business. Be attentive. Be quiet. Be courteous. And don't litter. Carry away everything you bring.

If these are unnecessary admonitions—and they might seem so when so much is said about litter and polution, you will understand our concern the closer you look at our world, as you do on foot, you will appreciate how fragile it is. And because you will have so much enjoyment from it you will, we trust, admonish others to take care too.

Remember, if it's raining, it's a good day to walk. If it's cold or windy, or cold *and* windy, it's a good day to walk. Just dress for it. Taking a walk is almost always a good thing to do.

Rodney and Priscilla Albright

Contents

Former Estates

Salt Marshes and Fresh Water Creeks

Sand Spits and Points

North Shore Beaches

Short Walks on Long Island

1. Robert Moses State Park

Robert Moses State Park is the westernmost 1000 acres of Fire Island, and is reachable by car across causeway and bridge, which take you over Great South Bay and Fire Island Inlet, to several parking fields accommodating over 5000 cars. It is parkway all 49 miles from New York City.

Walkable any time of year, you will never be alone hiking this broad flat beach. It is something of an adventure, because its ready accessibility draws a wide assortment of people attracted here by the sea, the sand, the spaciousness of its open sky. But it is refreshing. Breathing air tempered by the sea, observing others revelling in the out of doors, and alert to the sandpipers scurrying to surf's edge but wheeling away into the air as you approach, always keeping a distance from you, somehow time will pass more quickly than you'd imagine. So look at your watch as you leave the parking area. There is uninterrupted beach ahead for 31 miles. More than you can walk today.

From the easternmost large parking lot the distances are:
East to the Lighthouse 1.4 miles
East to Kismet (first Fire Island community) 2.1 miles
East to The Sunken Forest 6.7 miles
West to Lookout Tower at Fire Island Inlet 3.4 miles

Although Fire Island, stretching from Bay Shore to Center Moriches, is 31 miles long, in some places it is only 300 yards wide. There are eighteen developed communities here on the island, but aside from these, the U. S. Government

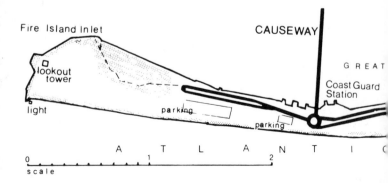

has acquired the remaining land and now administers the area, adhering to conservationist principles, as a National Seashore, somewhat the equivalent of a National Park. Three ranger stations are at Sailor's Haven (near the Sunken Forest), Watch Hill (near Davis Park), where camping is permitted, and the Administrative Office is in Patchogue just west of the Suffolk County Park at Smith's Point.

The beach, known for many years as Great South Beach, is indeed great, one of the finest beaches in the world. As you come at different seasons you will see that it changes size and shape, is cut away in winter, flattens out in summer. Erosion brings change as does the longshore transport of sand by currents. The Lighthouse, which was originally built in 1825 on the western tip of the island, is now five miles inland, and the Robert Moses State Park is growing at the rate of about 300 ft. a year!

For a short walk head out eastward. We clock ourselves, going for about an hour, then turn around and come back, and advise you to do the same. You will probably get to the Lighthouse or a bit beyond.

Perhaps it is best, if you seek solitude, to walk here after a storm or during the rain when most people will not venture afield. But people flock together and groups thin out as you go eastward.

There are refreshment stands, picnic shelters and a bathhouse open in season.

ROBERT MOSES STATE PARK

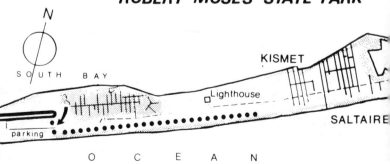

2. Sailor's Haven—Sunken Forest

To reach the Sailor's Haven Ranger Station, take the ferry from Sayville. If you can arrange it and have the stamina, you can get a ferry at Patchogue to Davis Park, then walk along the beach westward to Sailor's Haven, a distance of 6.5 miles, returning by ferry to Sayville.

The waves of the great Atlantic Ocean, set in motion 600 or more miles offshore by the wind, head westward unimpeded, slide up over the continental shelf and, with almost hourly changes of mood, strike the Long Island south shore beaches with pulsations of fascinating and hypnotic qualities. Its visual aspects change too, so frequently in fact, that there is never a dull day at the beach. There is never the threat of oppressive crowds. It is glorious. There is a fascination that nothing can quite describe, drawing you back again and again, refreshing you—and quietly luring you into spending an hour or a day longer than you had in mind.

We have come in the early spring, starting off in weather so thick we could not see Fire Island from the Sayville side, to have the sun later break through to show off the carpet of beach heather climbing these dunes, golden in bloom.

As the barrier beach built up, collecting more and more sand, the wind piled it up and formed these dunes. While some are only four or five feet high, many, as these here, reach a height of 35 or 40 feet. Behind the dunes here, between Cherry Grove and Point O'Woods, is a sanctuary well worth a visit and which affords a pleasant walk. It is the

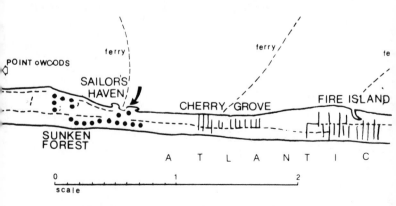

Sunken Forest, which has pretty close to 600 ft. of frontage on the beach, and comprises almost 40 acres of land. It is a short walk, close at hand to the Sailor's Haven ferry dock. As you cross to the south and climb the ramps protecting the dunes, you rise 35 ft. above sea level and look across the top of the dunes to the Great South Bay beyond.

The dense vegetation between you and the Bay is the top of the forest. Now almost unique, although there have been many similar forests in New Jersey as well as Cape Cod, the Sunken Forest of Fire Island has fortunately been preserved, and we are able to see here many trees which are estimated to be a hundred years old. The principal trees are holly, tupelo and sassafras, grown to a height of 35 to 40 ft. Normally these species do not reach this size because they are crowded out by stronger, taller growing trees. Here, however, the red maple, red cedar, black and post oak, and pitch pine are themselves sheared off by the winds from the ocean, thus are stunted to the protecting screen height of the dunes. It is dense with the tangles of wild grape, catbrier, a floor of ferns, Canada mayflower and false solomon's seal.

Descending the path into this primitive forest you have an unusual experience. It is similar to being in a jungle, and interesting too because of the land birds. The path comes out on the bay side into almost blinding light if it is a bright day, through thickets of plume grass, hugs the sandy shore, and reenters the forest to the west, twining back through the area. On a hot summer day it's pleasantly cool.

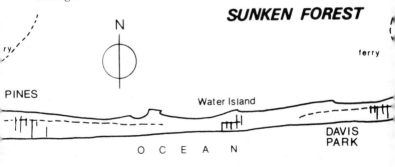

SUNKEN FOREST

N

ry

ferry

PINES

Water Island

OCEAN

DAVIS PARK

3. Smith Point—National Seashore

The beach accessible at Smith's Point is one of our favorite places to walk. At the south end of the William Floyd Parkway a causeway and toll bridge cross to the eastern end of the island, where there's ample parking space. Train service on the Montauk line goes to Shirley. From the Shirley station to the bridge it's two and a half miles. The toll charge across the bridge is seventy-five cents.

Two geodesic domes on the dunes house the National Seashore ranger's office, which are open in summer months and contain an informative display on beach life. Rangers guide interesting short walks from here.

Head out in either direction. East to Moriches Inlet is 4.2 miles, a long hike there and back. West is stretchable as far as your legs can carry you. We usually go a little over two miles to the Old Inlet Clubhouse, a private swimming club tucked away in the dunes, and return. In moderate or cold weather it's nice to come back on the jeep road running inland parallel to the ocean.

At low tide pebbles are exposed which, in their wet state, get you started on a pebble collection! There are white ones and black, red ones and brown, lavender and with subtle variations, a seemingly limitless selection. In fact that's where all the sand comes from, from the rocks and stones beating against each other, reducing themselves into smaller and smaller pieces, sand being the smallest particles to which

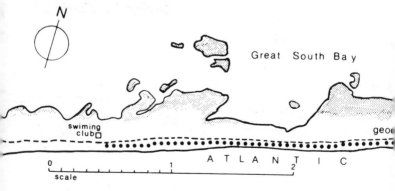

they are ever reduced. Scoop up these dry sands and as they run through your fingers investigate them carefully. At least half the sand is quartz, but there is horneblende, rutile, feldspar, augite, magnetite, ilmenite—a variety of names to confound you, or just possibly to start you exploring a whole new world of minerals and rock. Below Hatteras, down into the beaches of the South much of the sand is made up of tiny shell fragments, but not here on Long Island. Shells are relatively scarce. The rocks which make up these beaches were brought by the mighty glaciers of the ice age all the way from Canada. So as you inspect the debris of the sand you might find anything. They tell me specks of ruby and emerald exist here—but rarely! However, if you search, you'll certainly find garnet, and the black patches contain magnetite, an important ore sometimes possessing polarity, when it does, called lodestone. If you run a magnet through this, you'll find particles will cling.

With no people living on this thin stretch of the barrier beach, a walk here exposes some of the fragile links in the chain of life. For among the variety of life zones—the tidal edge of the sea, the beach itself, behind the sandy swales of the dunes, and in the wetlands along the Great South Bay— is a busy world to capture your interest and excite your imagination. We see hoof prints of deer here often, but deer are remarkable in becoming invisible. Only once or twice have we actually seen them here, and then what a thrill!

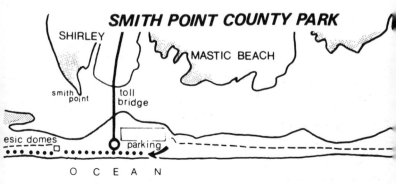

4. Westhampton Beach

Now, since almost the entire stretch is privately owned, access to the beaches is limited if you have no local connections. The western tip at Moriches, however, is county owned, and although the parking area maintained there is limited to Suffolk County residents in summer months, we have frequently walked here off season.

To reach this western tip you drive south from the Montauk Highway on Mill Road, right on, and to the end of, Main Street through the town of Westhampton, then left, on Potunk Lane, and follow Jessup Lane across the bridge, then turn right on Dune Road. Thence it is 4.5 miles west to the end of the road. From here along the edge of the ocean the distance to the jetty at Moriches Inlet is 1.5 miles. The surf can be formidable, crashing and spuming; there has been some geysering here on a couple of occasions when we've walked! Because the point is without habitations it can be marvellously wild. We turn north at the jetty and walk back along the inlet to the quieter waters on Moriches Bay. Offshore the islands are breeding areas for skimmers and terns, and you should be stealthy and alert for this is an especially good birding spot for larger shore birds and wanderers. The sand is firm and you'll find secluded pockets to stretch out to relax if you wish. Then, after continuing northeastward for a quarter of a mile, you'll find a road leading up from the water to the center of the dunes and to

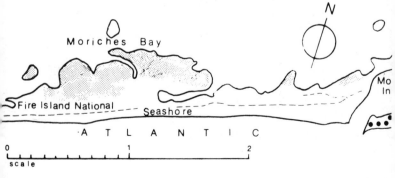

another road paralleling the ocean, which will bring you back to the parking lot. These grassy dunes are spacious, and filled with interdune plant and wild life. In the summer months they can be too hot for comfort, but out of season they are magnificent, and late in the day the low light gives them the Elvira Madigan look, which is so romantic.

In September 1938 when the hurricane hit this beach, it had not been anticipated. Thunderstorms occurred the night before. But next morning everyone set about his business as usual. Heavy rain didn't start until 1pm, and winds reached 45 mph. By 3 o'clock the situation became critical, a gale was howling, and water was all over the beach. The center of the storm hit Westhampton before other places to the east. The tide was 10 to 15 feet above normal, and the sea beat at, and broke through, the dunes. Only the higher ones or stronger bulkheads held. New inlets were cut through into Quantuck and Shinnecock Bays. From Mecox to Saga-ponac Pond, the ocean broke through at five places!

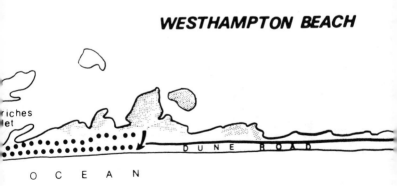

WESTHAMPTON BEACH

Cross the bridge at Quogue or Hampton Bays on to Dune Road. About midway between the two is Tiana Beach, where there's parking and easy access across the dunes.

Wide and open, the beach here is strung out with cottages all along behind the dunes, but not dominating the landscape. We generally walk a mile west, by the round apartment complex and several summer places to the beachhouse maintained by the village of Quogue, and return. Then we walk another mile east to total an hour and a half, or two hours of elapsed time. It is never too crowded.

Low tide is the best time to walk on the beach, because the wet sand is compacted and settled by the waves so all along the water's edge the firm walkway is hard enough not to hold you back in your own footsteps. Actually, water still remains between the individual grains of sand and even on the hottest days the sun only dries the surface. There's a microscopic world of channels and ponds teeming with almost invisible life. Just watch the tiny sandpipers scurrying up to the water's edge pecking away into the oozing sand. That's what they're after.

Quite apart from our walks, however, there is another reason compelling us to come back here. That is Dune Road. The variety of shore birds using the wetlands along the north of the road is almost endless. Almost all these creatures who nest or visit Long Island can be seen at some spot along

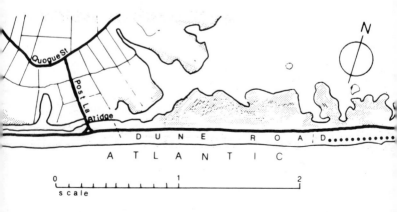

here, wading in the shallows, standing in the grass, or winging low over the water. During the migratory season you will see one or two dunlin, black bellied plover, ruddy turnstone, and then another and another, until you realize that the grass or shoreline is alive with them.

Come equipped with glasses and your bird guide. You'll find your car a perfect blind from which to observe. Drive along slowly. We've seen and heard the clapper rail with his raucous call; seen the bittern, watched him slowly swaying as he holds his bill in the air pretending to be a reed, trying to elude us. And we have watched black skimmer after black skimmer feeding, with their precision glide along the water. You'll see it all on Dune Road.

The wetlands swarm with insects, are slimy, the water unfit to drink. But acre for acre, the salt marsh will produce more plants than any farm, fertilizing itself, needing no help from man in planting or harvesting. Not only is it the feeding grounds for migrating birds you see along Dune Road, but it provides shelter and food for small mammals as well. We've watched the muskrat swimming here and working in the shallows, for example. And the tiny fish that swim and breed here are carried out on tides to feed still larger fish miles from shore. When you see the filling in of some of this wetland, you realize that there are still some who have not got the message.

TIANA BEACH

PONQUOGUE BRIDGE

S h i n n e c o c k B a y

O C E A N

6. Southampton Beach

From the Shinnecock Inlet in Southampton eastward, the beach stretches in a broad unbroken swath for eleven miles to Sagaponack Pond. In summer this area attracts for the most part those who are content to lie out in the sun, dip in the magnificent surf—sometimes it's too magnificent and must be respected—and picnic, or fling the frisbee. Off season it is almost completely uninhabited except for the occasional dog walker, surf fisherman or bird watcher.

There are many places of public access where you may park. Sometimes there is a fee or a parking permit is required (obtained at the Southampton Town Hall). Out of season, however, there is no problem.

This stretch is characterized by high dunes, rather large summer houses, set usually well behind the dunes for protection, a number of guarded beaches for swimming, good walking at low tide, and many ponds just behind the dunes where there is always more to be seen than a bird. At the east end of Shinnecock Bay the beach ceases to be a barrier island, (or here a peninsula), and all the rest of the way to Montauk becomes part of the mainland. These are classic beaches, the kind you see in marvelous color prints, the dunes covered with pale chartreuse grasses and, over the broad stretches of white sand, a mist of salt spray, the sun catching the movement of the waves.

At the Shinnecock or western end of this stretch there are

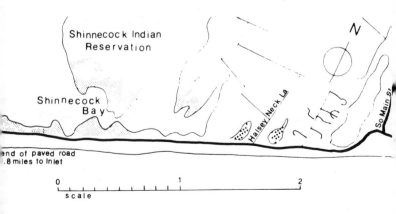

no buildings at all and the dunes are unusually high. Terns must nest here, for once when here in the spring they literally dive-bombed us. Parking out here is informal. The road peters out, so be careful unless you have a 4-wheel drive vehicle. The walk to the jetty is about two miles.

There are three or four other accesses to the beach. Our favorite section to walk is the one locally known as Fowlers. The approach to the high dunes is through broad potato fields, some seasons planted to wheat for rotation. The parking is along one side of the lane, so your walk is first to get to the beach, looking for wild things near the ponds. On both sides they usually have interesting birds. And in August they are surrounded by huge pink or rose flowers of the pink mallow. We turn left as we come onto the beach, walk along the water to Mecox Bay and back, making a total distance of just over three miles, comfortable for us and includes the goal of getting to the big bay to watch sailboats or see if we can spot a long billed dowitcher lurking in the shallows. The surfing must be pretty good for there is always a young crowd there complete with boards and wet suits. And, incidently, in winter there is ice boating on Mecox Bay.

Beach walks clear your mind of many things. Often personal problems are replaced by other thoughts like those stemming from the fact that geologists say these beaches are a million years old!

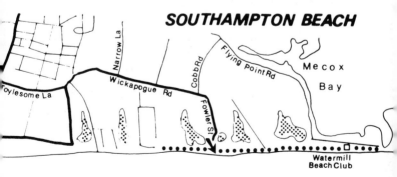

SOUTHAMPTON BEACH

7. Wainscott Beach

Of the five unbroken stretches of beach along Long Island's south shore, Wainscott Beach, 3.6 miles from end to end, is the shortest. Many walkers have a compulsion to cover every mile of a stretch, just because it is there, and its easy to understand the urge because there is a satisfaction to having traversed any stretch. Still, on the broad flat strands of the coastline here, there isn't a startling surprise of discovery. One beach is very much like another. There are differences, of course, but these differences are subtle, sometimes more metaphysical than real. And since, from hour to hour, aspects of the beach walking experience changes anyway, it can be misleading to describe any of Long Island's beaches in specific details. Wainscott Beach is probably the most out of the way. There are cottages all along, well back in grassy stretches. The dunes are lower. For some reason driftwood does not accumulate here to the extent it does farther east. Freighters at sea seem farther out.

To reach Wainscott Beach, turn south from the Montauk Highway 3 miles east of Bridgehampton on Main Street to Sagaponack, and on to the end; or to the end of Beach Lane in Wainscott.

It's a good idea to check the tide tables before you start off and try to do your principal walking during the low tide, when the footing is more solid and the walking easier! Up on the higher ground the surface sand does dry to a greater depth and walking becomes more laborious.

When you stand on the beach facing the sea you can notice from many little indicators that the water pulls to the west. For the longest time we simply couldn't understand this. We'd say that the gulf stream was out there moving eastward and northward along the coast, so how could the water here along shore move as it obviously does, in the opposite direction? Have you asked yourself this question? Have you seen how the sand moves with the currents west, how pieces of driftwood move back toward New York? In a word the answer is friction. The gulf stream is a very large river, about forty miles wide and two thousand feet deep, with a volume of water a thousand times larger than our biggest river, and it moves about 5.5 miles per hour in a northeasterly direction. As it moves, the water along the shore is set into currents and eddys which flow for a time in the reverse direction because of the friction of the shore.

From Georgica Pond the Long Island South beach is uninterrupted for 22.2 miles to Montauk. Locally the stretch is referred to by calling it East Hampton Beach, Amagansett Beach, Napeague Beach or Montauk Beach, depending on its proximity to the adjoining community. The entire stretch is magnificent and eminently walkable.

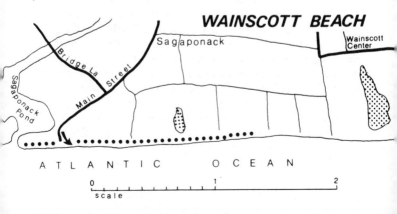

8. East Hampton Beach

Parking on East Hampton beaches is restricted to residents only during the season. East Hampton is chic, as a town, beautifully maintained, handsome because of tree shaded lanes and many attractive houses; has a casual dignity and considerable local civic pride. We've driven along streets here early in the morning, before breakfast, on the way to the beach, and seen golden pheasant, one after another, strutting across village greenswards. This pastoral, relaxed village atmosphere is the secret of East Hampton's jealously guarded charm, and a strong effort is being made to keep it this way.

A good walk on the East Hampton beach is from the town beach east of Hook Pond walking westward to the Georgica Pond inlet and return. The total distance, round trip, is 6.4 miles. The Maidstone Golf Club will be on your right as you head out, also Hook Pond, which is a good birding area. Beyond Main Street Beach the dune area is fairly primitive, low and windswept. Off season you can find a place to park.

The beach here is in striking contrast to, say, the beaches west of Jones Beach, where our urban sprawl has crowded out the dunes. The charm and attractiveness of Eastern Long Island is threatened by growth—the statistically predictable population explosion and overcrowding which seems inevitable. East Hampton is vigorously trying to preserve its heritage, limit its growth, save its open land for living space. The East End Chapter of the Nature Conservancy is an active one. Acres of land have been saved through its efforts. As you walk Long Island you will appreciate its openness, see the need to save its wild areas, but feel the pressures crowding in to crush its rural character. You may feel yourself helpless as an individual in a crowded society, and may ask yourself what you can do to help in conserving this. The answer seems to be to become involved, to work with others for a common end. The administration of our civic affairs apparently works only under pressure of an aroused citizenry.

One organization concerned is the Nature Conservancy, whose Long Island Chapter can be contacted through PO Box 72, Cold Springs Harbor, New York 11724. Family membership is $15, or $10 for a subscribing member.

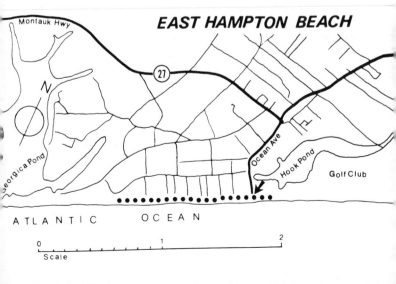

9. Amagansett Beach

An easy direct access to Amagansett Beach is to turn south off the Montauk Highway on Indian Wells Highway (just out of East Hampton but before you reach Amagansett) which takes you there. At its end is a bath house on the east side, and opposite this, Sheppard's Dunes, an eight acre area acquired and protected by the Nature Conservancy to preserve its natural state. Parking during the season is reserved for residents. It's better to walk in late spring or early fall anyway.

The beach itself has character. Houses sit almost half a mile up from the beach on bluffs overlooking the sea, and the dunes are wild. So our suggestion is to walk to Maidstone Golf Club, which is 2.5 miles to the west on the wide beach, then return.

For anyone who has lived in inland wooded areas the plants and ground cover of the seashore offer a fascinating world of discovery. When there's a break in the dunes, as there is here, you can be tempted to cross in order to examine interior plant life. But don't do it. You will crush the dune grasses, make the passage vulnerable to wind erosion. And just one such spot can actually weaken an entire dune. So be conservation minded, and alert to any damage to any plant life. You will be able to find a path allowing you to observe.

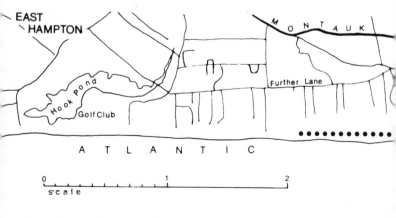

The beach grass with its long curving leaves is the principal stabilizer for the dunes. It gets its nourishment from wind blown minerals, grows up, sends its roots deep, follows the contours of the dunes. The false heather is another, with bright buttery yellow blossoms from May through July. It is a low shrubby plant adapted to life on the shifting sands.

Just over the dunes, when there's soil enough the beach pea will take hold, send its vine-like leaflets swarming, the ends with little tendrils like a pig's tail. You will want to examine the pea flowers which are delicate in shades of violet and purple, blossoming throughout the summer. Inland, thickets of beach plum and bayberry take hold with beautiful fruit in the fall.

When the dunes are stabilized it is amazing the exuberance that nature displays. Above all you should beware the poison ivy, rampant near the beach. You will find rugosa rose, seaside goldenrod, thistle and blueberry. It is really quite startling to realize the wide variety there is in plant life near the beach.

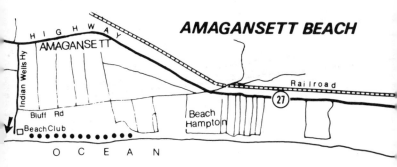

After you leave Amagansett, driving east, the ocean comes into view from the highway for the first time. The peninsula abruptly narrows, two bodies of water—Napeague Bay and Harbor—extend southward making the land here less than a mile wide until you reach Hither Hills, or for about 6 miles. The road parallels the ocean about a half mile inland. The land is flat with low dunes and with seaside plants with which you are familiar. The beach extending eastward from Amagansett is Napeague Beach. It's easiest to get on to the beach through the Hither Hills State Park.

Out here is a good place to get a feeling for the forces that shaped Long Island's topographical features. As you leave, you see Amagansett, the high dunes petering out, then at Hither Hills how the land mass piles up again, now in contours and hills that are over 150 ft. above sea level here. The land masses are the result of the swath pushed and dumped here by the glaciers, and the beaches are resultant from the continuous action, ever since, of wind and sea. Great rolling breakers have been moving in on the Long Island shoreline for a million years since the first glacier came down, and for over 25,000 years since the last, scooping up rocks and sand, rubbing and grinding and depositing the fine, fine particles, forming the present continuous beach. And wind has blown it around. What with storms and tides and longshore transit of sands by currents, there have been constant changes in elevations and shore lines. It is recorded

NAPEAG
HA

MONTAUK HIGHWAY

27

A   T   L   A   N   T   I   C

0   1   2

scale

that there were seven inlets east of Fire Island in 1743—but then Fire Island was 55 miles long. It was not until 1931 that big waves and high tides separated the dunes and broke through Fire Island at Moriches Inlet in a destructive storm. And it is inevitable that there will be further change.

As you walk the Napeague Beach, go east for a time and see the high bluffs where the southern moraine comes right to the sea. Turn around and walk past the Park to the low dunes. Along the way you will surely see a fisherman or two.

An underwater sand bar extends almost the entire length of the island about a quarter mile offshore, formed by the undertow. And you will generally see commercial and sport fishing boats trolling along over this bar. The fishing is apt to be good. At least surf casters have this attitude. During the summer there are schools of bluefish, sea bass, porgies and flounder. Late in the autumn striped bass can be caught and, through the winter, cod.

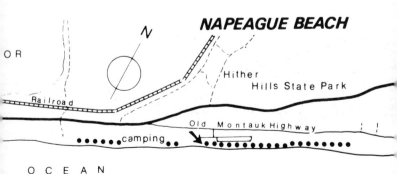

11. Montauk Beach

There's a gap in the morainal hills which is properly Montauk Beach, about a 3.5 mile stretch of broad sandy beach, from the high dunes along the Old Montauk Highway to the US Coast Guard Reservation. East of this you come to the seventy foot high bluffs, a kind of Landsend, halfway between New York City and the farthest reach of Cape Cod, which is Montauk Point. There are places to park right in town, and easy access. The beach is nice and wide. There will be bathers and people lying in the sun, if it's summer. And if you walk west towards the dunes you should surely see surfers in wet suits, because the conditions are evidently good there.

The kind of waves on which surfboarders get the best ride are known as spilling breakers—or those which, as they approach the beach, have a line of foam spilling down their front, always just about to break but holding off for quite a while. Since the more gradual the slope of the bottom, the longer the wave will hold off breaking, it stands that the best surfing is on that kind of beach which has a long stretch underwater with almost no slope at all.

There is never a day on these waters when there is no surf whatsoever, though it is possible it can be too dull for those who make a sport of it. The whole science of waves is complex, but it is interesting to know that a wave will break when the ratio of the height of the wave to the depth

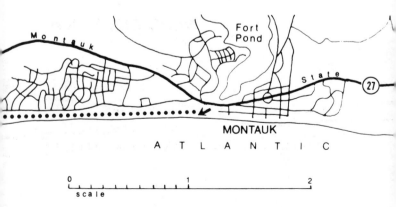

of water is about three to four; that is to say that a six foot wave will break in about eight feet of water.

The wave action is caused principally by the wind's force against the surface of the water. The water itself actually moves very little. You can see this when you watch a cork or piece of driftwood bobbing at sea, and after the wave has passed, how little the cork has moved. When a wave passes through very shallow waters it lifts and stirs up sand from the bottom, so the loose grains of sand settle in a place different from where it started. That's how waves change and shape the contours of beaches.

The changes in the beach would not, most likely, startle the Montauk Indians whose name it bears, and who were so naturally protected here from their mainland enemies, and who made quantities of wampum on these beaches from the shells of periwinkles and quahogs. Not startle them half so much as the changes on land, where the indigenous hardwoods of New England, beech, oak and maple, and of the 140 or 150 ft. tulip trees from which they fashioned their canoes, have all been destroyed.

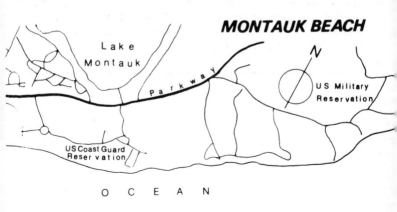

Towns To Do On Foot

One of the joys of walking is to step out of the fetters of time, to while away and unwind at a leisurely pace, and with a certain detachment. Keeping alert to the surroundings in this carefree state, there is a satisfaction which, when walking along the edge of the sea, becomes a kind of leap back in time to first beginnings and, in walking along narrow streets of an old village, becomes nostalgic, feeds our hankerings for a simpler life.

Long Island was colonized by New Englanders, mostly from Connecticut, and English architectural influences are visible in a number of places as far back as the Old House in Cutchogue. There are Dutch influences too which pushed eastward from New Amsterdam.

Rural village charms that still exist on Long Island are mainly left over from the nineteenth century. By then the settlement had established a character which has strong appeals to us today; appeals that have been trampled over in mass invasions of real estate development throughout the western area. And these, in a creeping urbanization, threaten to take over still more of the island.

12. Sag Harbor

Sag Harbor is certainly one of the best preserved old villages on Long Island, with hedges and picket fences, curving and shaded streets which are lined with charming houses.

Starting at the waterfront, walk along Bay Avenue and on to the long wharf, observe the coastal activity and inspect the waterfront, shop at one of the ship chandlers catering to yachtsmen if you wish, and from the bridge look across the harbor toward Shelter Island. Then walk up Main Street as far as you like. The Greek Revival edifice built in 1845, now housing the Whaling and Historical Museum is a point of interest (though its exhibits are less than outstanding), on up and across the street from the museum is the Hannibal House, a large Victorian house now painted a pleasant green color, also the old Customs House, now a National Landmark, the home and office of the first customs collector of New York State. George Washington, in 1797, named Sag Harbor an official Port of Entry to the United States.

On side streets—wander off on any of them—you'll see many fine little houses built during prosperous days, late 18th to mid-19th century. They have simple lines and the style of that era. These residential streets today, since many of the houses have been restored with care, painted and nicely planted by their present owners, give you the feeling of the prosperity of the past.

Eventually you should turn left and go over to Madison Street between Main and Union Streets, to see the Whalers Church, based on Egyptian style and something of a curiosity, but now lacking the spyglass shaped steeple that once dominated the town, blown down in the hurricane of 1938 and never replaced. All the architectural trim is said to be hand carved by whalers from the village. And nearby, the old graveyard is interesting. A lovelier looking church is Christ Episcopal down the street. Sag Harbor is a place with a special atmosphere.

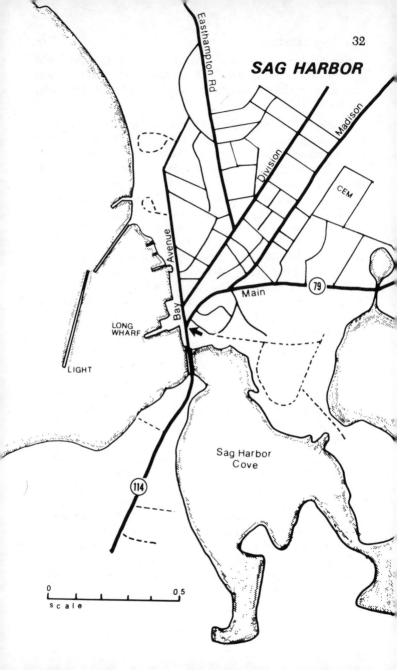

SAG HARBOR

Easthampton Rd

Madison

Division

CEM

79

Main

Avenue

Bay

LONG
WHARF

LIGHT

Sag Harbor
Cove

114

0   0.5
s c a l e

First there was a little fishing village started here in 1697 by a small band of Narragansetts, traditional rivals of the Montauks and Shinnecocks. Then the white settlers moved in around 1730. Although known for a time as Sterling Bay (after the English Lord Sterling), it eventually took the name Sag Harbor, being the harbor of Sagg, a little settlement near what is now Bridgehampton, a contraction of the Indian place name Saggabonac: "Place of Nut Grounds."

At the end of the 18th century Sag Harbor cleared a greater tonnage of goods than New York Harbor, and it was to become one of the principal whaling ports on the Atlantic seacoast. Between 1790 and 1870 over 500 voyages were made from here and the whale oil brought back to light the cities and houses of New England was valued at $25 million. There were once 63 vessels registered here. The population reached 3500 by 1843. Rough seamen walked these very streets you roam today. Montauk and Shinnecock Indians, but also Fiji Islanders, Hawaiians, Malays, Ethiopians and Portugese. Clearly no princely fortunes were amassed here, as in Nantucket to the Macys and Folgers, because voyages were financed as joint stock company ventures.

After the Civil War the whaling industry had a rapid decline and Sag Harbor's fortunes dwindled.

13. Old Bethpage Village

Old Bethpage Village is a restoration, a composite made up of simple houses with some architectural merit, regrouped here on a 200 acre site ample enough to provide a proper setting for the buildings, and recreate the atmosphere of a mid-nineteenth century village. And it is a pleasant surprise. We think it makes a delightful walk, a lovely switch in centuries. Still not complete at this writing, for the summer's day we walked around the village eighteen buildings were here, and we were able to walk through ten of them. Eventually the plan is to have a total of thirty.

You will find a parking lot and the Nassau County Museum, of contemporary design. Here there is an adequate cafeteria, an excellent gift shop, and a small auditorium showing film on the restoration. The admission is $1.50 for adults, half fare for children. Allow a couple of hours, and spend another if you can make the time.

We walked into the days before the mechanization of the farm. This illusion is skillfully achieved. The dirt path we followed is bordered by a post and rail fence, the field through which it ambled lay fallow, but liberally sprinkled with Queen Anns lace and butterflies. Birds chirped. There was the faint, not unpleasant, organic smell that emanates from a farmyard.

We were greeted at the first house by an eager youth who showed us through. It had been a bayman's dwelling. Uncluttered, simply furnished, it set an informal friendly air to our visit.

At the crossroads is a general store, with the proprietor's living quarters under the same roof, an Inn serving Birch Beer in the Tap Room, and a Blacksmith's forge. By this time we had noticed that all the guides were dressed in clothes of the period. It is not correct to say that they were wearing costumes—the garb is simple, functional and doesn't at first catch your eye.

The farm is functioning. There are pigs and cows, chickens

OLD BETHPAGE

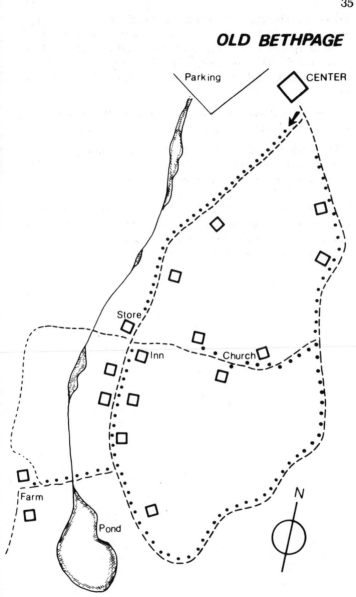

and geese. The ladies were baking bread and a pot of soup hung simmering from the crane over coals smoldering away in the fireplace. It was vegetable soup and the gardens had provided all the ingredients. The flies buzzed, a Canada goose honked, and the old sow lay sprawled out in the mud.

It is an uncluttered, friendly, helpful little valley, and the attitude of all the people working here make it so.

The walk around the loop is 1.5 miles. During the school year we were told there are daily groups—so our suggestion is to come, as we did, on a summer's day. Let the natural breezes provide the stream to float your daydreams on. Lengthen your stride, but slow down your pace, and reflect how downright simple the necessities of life can be. The mile and a half walk, plus the other exploring footsteps will add up to enough on a hot afternoon.

"The style of the houses in Sea Cliff," says one local resident with a measure of civic pride, "is what we call 'Carpenter Gothic.' " Perhaps this sets in your mind's eye a village which is a collection of highly individual gingerbread houses on which personal effort has been applied over the years. Actually there's an ample supply of larger, well maintained Victorian ones as well. You should enjoy a walk in Sea Cliff for surprises! It rolls comfortably over high bluffs overlooking the Hempstead Harbor. Narrow streets running up and down steep slopes, some very small parcels of land, and loving care, are the complementary parts which make up a whole picture of Sea Cliff which forms as you trudge around the town on foot.

Start off by parking near Clifton Park, and walk along westward on Sea Cliff Avenue. There are some big houses here, and you'll cross through the business district, perhaps quickly sensing that the principal industry is selling antiques these days. Eventually you will reach Memorial Park, site of the old Battershall Inn, which was demolished by the town for back taxes. The property is on the heights and you will come upon a grand view of the Long Island Sound. Across in Westchester is the town of Rye; on your left is Port Washington.

Walk north on Prospect Avenue, left down Cliffway, and north again on Boulevard. Two sets of steps will bring you back up to Prospect. An alternate longer walk, is to go from Memorial Park down Prospect Avenue to the shoreline and follow it south as it curves along under the lovely old plane trees to Scudders Pond. Returning, you can explore the narrow streets along Sea Cliff's "Cliff Side."

The first gathering of people here was really a Methodist summer "Camp Meeting" with tents, picnics and summer smiles on faces of earnest city folk, singing hymns on the wooded hills above the water, away from the ruffians of the city. That was in 1865. Good steamboat service to New

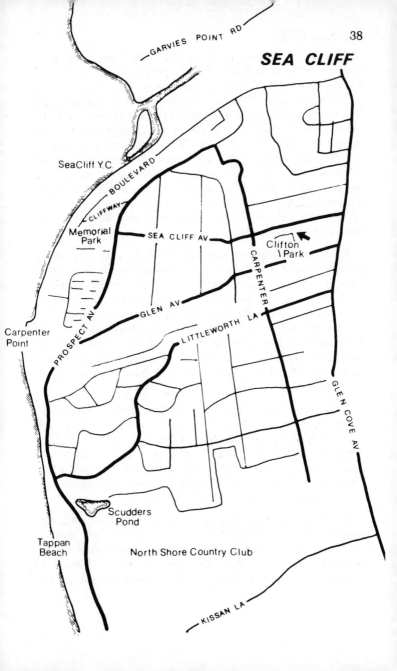

SEA CLIFF

York City was available and convenient from the pier in the harbor. They later bought 240 acres from the Carpenter family who owned the farmlands and divided it. This atmosphere was as so congenial that people eventually built little houses on their 40 x 60 tent lots to make it more permanent, and lavished every spare dollar they could to make it attractive.

By 1895 however, its charms having spread, it had become a very popular summer resort; large Victorian houses had been built. There was a cable car up the cliff and a board walk had been built along the shore front. The Long Island Railroad was running trains into the little gingerbread station on a regular schedule spring, summer and fall, as well as four boats, daily and Sunday, between Sea Cliff and New York.

The incorporated village is just a mile square, and its present middleclass owners with civic mindedness have preserved and protected its character from encroachments all around. It probably stands today as one of the best preserved little square miles around.

15. Stony Brook

Because Stony Brook is old, handsome, has a lovely setting and several points of interest, we have included it here as a short walk, although it is not laid out on a grid plan and doesn't have extensive sidewalks. Therefore, the amount of exploring possible here on foot is somewhat limited. We think that you should see it, though, for its unique charm and Long Island bayside country atmosphere.

Our suggestion is that you go directly to the Old Carriage Museum, which is on Route 25A at Main Street, and park your car there, or if you come by train, that this should be your starting point. There is an admission charge of $1.50, and the place is indescribably fascinating. If you haven't thought much about old carriages (and who has?) then you are in for some surprises. This collection, displayed in a perfect setting, is mind boggling. Carts, cabs, coaches, broughams, phaetons, wagons are assembled here that are sure to delight you, no matter how uninterested you may think you are in a collection of old carriages! Man's ingenious capacity to build and skill in handling materials, his inventiveness in problem solving are the basic proficiencies on display, and which startle you into a consciousness of the continuity of civilization. Besides carriages there is a blacksmith's shop, a schoolhouse and a printshop to walk through, all preserved from the 19th century.

When you have seen enough, walk north along the sidewalk .5 miles into the village, skirting the pond which has a great blue heron, families of ducks, waterlilies and beautiful shade trees. It also supplies the power for an old grist mill at its head.

As you come into town the harbor will be on your left, so walk along to the dock. The bay and spartina meadows here supply as New England a setting to view as any you might imagine. And the waters are lively. It is not difficult to see how the English settlers who came here from Suffolk chose these shores, or why it reminded them of their native

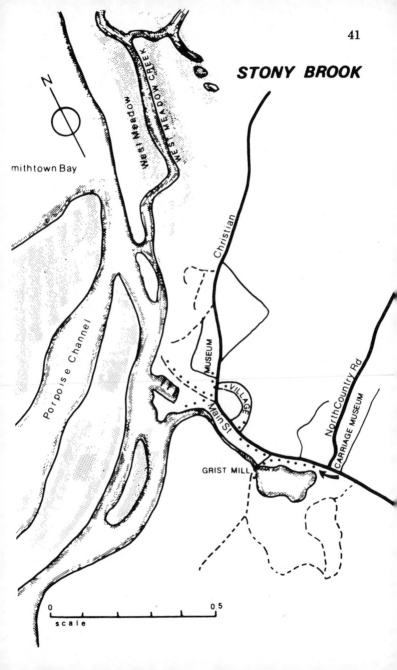

STONY BROOK

N

mithtown Bay

WEST MEADOW

WEST MEADOW CREEK

Porpoise Channel

Christian

MUSEUM

VILLAGE

Main St

GRIST MILL

North Country Rd

CARRIAGE MUSEUM

0   0.5
scale

county. It is easy to understand too, here, the overwhelmingly important part played by the sea, the bays and water routes in the first two hundred years of the development of Long Island.

At the head of the village is a small Suffolk Museum which has a pretty collection of ship models and upstairs, in a glassed case, a bird collection.

The village is clean and tidy and preserves an air. You can walk along window-shopping and head back to your starting point, but surely you will have lost track of time along the way.

Another point of interest, on Nicoll Road south from Stony Brook is the new campus of the University of New York State, a complex of buildings which is enormous and will provide modern university facilities for over 15,000 students.

Places on earth, like people, seem to develop under current conditions along conforming lines. One airport looks pretty much like any other, anywhere in our world, and cities and houses fall into similar categories. Those exceptions that guard their character from external forces, which have tendencies to change it, and preserve their antiquities, develop an aura which is often admirable. Little villages lying somewhere along headwaters tend to preserve this aura, and Orient Village, lying the farthest east of any of the villages on the northern fluke, quite off the beaten track, has perhaps the greatest individuality of anyplace on Long Island. We hope, in saying this, that anyone will cautiously consider the trust we place in him who reads this. Don't rush right out to look. A swarm of people would be out of place in Orient. Also it is a simple place, you won't be overwhelmed! The houses aren't grand as they are in Southampton or East Hampton. Property plots are rather small, and the antiquities are not on a scale that would attract Sotheby's. It is not quaint, and there are no shops of any kind, other than a small general store and post office, closed Sundays. So you might be disappointed. But for us, Orient has a special character, all its own.

If you go, you will leave Greenport on Route 25. The town of East Marion is 2 or 3 miles, and beyond that 3.3 miles, just after you cross the narrow causeway with the Long Island Sound on your left and Orient Harbor on your right, is the road which leads down into the village. As you come to this causeway you should stop at a parking place along the harbor, get out and look. The map lays out well before you here. The village, from the distance, seems like one you'd see in Vermont. There are snowy white egrets which nest in the salt meadows and a peacefulness laid down on all the scene. We have read that Orient Village until after World War I was a favorite spot for honeymooners. Today it is primarily a quiet resort town. Don't try to drive into town. Park off the road near the war memorial and the white church

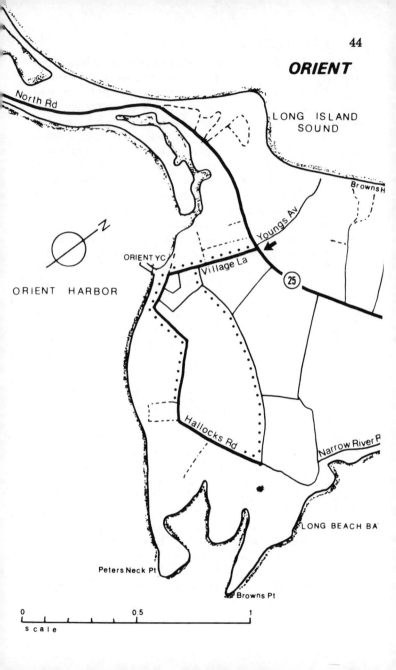

ORIENT

North Rd

LONG ISLAND
SOUND

Brownsl

Youngs Av

ORIENT YC

Village La

25

ORIENT HARBOR

Hallocks Rd

Narrow River P

LONG BEACH BA

Peters Neck Pt

Browns Pt

0   0.5   1

s c a l e

with the graceful steeple at the head of the lane. Then walk along the sidewalk. Houses, gardens, trees and reflections will catch your eye. Orient has over 100 buildings over 100 years old. Down the quiet, narrow, meandering Village Lane, is the four museum complex. This sounds formidable but isn't. There is the Village House Museum, a simple clapboard structure with a long widow's walk, and today run by the Oyster Ponds Historical Society. It has early American furnishings and local collections and is worth a visit in summer when open. Next door on a lawn is the Old School-house, across the street the Hallock House. Then there is the Red Barn, and so on. Continue down the lane by the yacht club, and you can lengthen the walk as we do by continuing on out into the country fields and swing back by a loop into the village.

17. Peconic River County Park (undeveloped)

South of the Middle Country Road and West of Calverton is a vast sparsely populated area, mostly woodland, which supports considerable wildlife. The woods we walk in here are used primarily by duck hunters during the fall hunting season. Deer are plentiful, and there are eight or nine small ponds.

A good access to these boggy ponds is an unmarked road 2.6 miles north of Long Island Expressway Exit 69 on Wading River Road, or 1.2 miles south on Wading River Road from Route 25, and just opposite Manor Road. It is a dirt road on each side of which the posted signs read "Cooperative Hunting Area," and which leads in about a half mile directly to Sandy Pond.

The half day or more you spend in this area will be peaceful—maybe a fisherman or camper will already be here, but we've met only one other hiker in the woods, though we've walked it many times. You'll find a place to park near Sandy Pond by the tumbling remains of a brick house. From here walk westward over the trail.

This is just east of the Brookhaven National Laboratory, and west of the Grumman Peconic River Airport, and is a long narrow strip of land on which Horn, Round, Peasys, Woodchoppers, Duck, Sandy, Grassy, Twin and Jones Pond follow one after another, north to south, and are each part of the chain of little ponds which form the stream that meanders to Riverhead, making the Peconic River the longest on Long Island. On this strip there are fire roads north to south, and crossing, and on which you can wander without getting lost, and on which, if you're wearing rubber boots, you can go safely anytime of year, except during the duck hunting season of mid-November through the first week in January. It's apt to be wet in spots.

Bird life abounds, and we've seen at least twenty different mushrooms over the years. Although we've rushed home

PECONIC RIVER

afterwards to look in our mushroom guide, we've never done more than photograph them. The great blue heron lives in Woodchoppers Pond. You'll see several species of duck, little green heron, a Canada goose family. In the spring warblers, the oriole, the scarlet tanager, partridge and woodcock. We were thrilled to identify positively the red crossbill among these pitch pine and oak. The shores of the ponds are marshy, and in the fall the colors are riotous.

For a woodland walk, quiet, rural and startlingly extensive, Muttontown Nature Preserve is ideal. It is an irregularly U-shaped parcel of land behind estates, its trails through the evergreen woods are bridle paths left over from days when all this was horsey country. Open to the public as a division of the Nassau County Museum, it is being allowed to go back to nature, and intelligently administered. Adjoining the property we describe is a still larger one fenced in and protected, and only open for group visits by arrangement, making all the more secluded walk, shielded from distractions and commotions caused by groups in our dense population.

The entrance to the preserve is at the end of Muttontown Lane, a little road running south off Route 25A, just west of East Norwich and Route 106. And there is a parking lot in front of a simple building, newly built, being developed as a Nature Center. Behind, is a little pond which was dug in 1967 to provide better drainage to the wet area here, and deciduous woods of swamp maple, swamp oak, and tupelo, the tree closely related to the sourgum of southern swamps, and which turns scarlet in autumn. Although the pond doesn't support any fish, it does provide the environment needed by a variety of beetles and flies, and attracts turtles, frogs and salamanders, as well as a variety of birds.

Happily the trails are marked with colored blazes, and this is most helpful to guide you along twisty, turny paths where otherwise you might miss seeing much the area offers. Many of the trees are marked too for identification. Watch out for poison ivy which grows rank throughout the preserve!

Follow the blue or green blazes through the swamp area where you will find arrowwood and spicebush growing, along with ferns, mosses and liverworts, and you will come out on a large field, once farmland, now let go so that it attracts bobwhite and pheasant, field mice and woodchuck, and turn right here following the green blazes into the

MUTTONTOWN PRESERVE

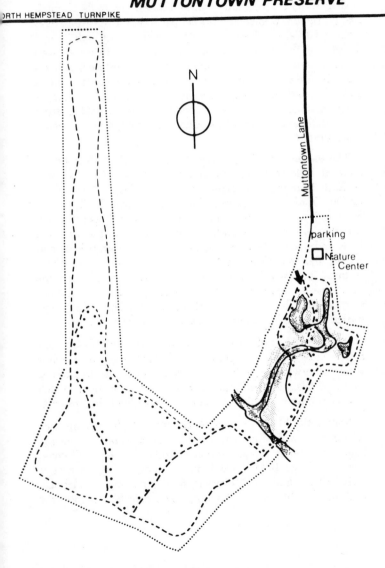

evergreen woods. On the hot summer day we walked here the cool of this woods was noticeable. It is a forest of white pine and larch, with a scattering of dogwood and black cherry, and paths are spongy, good walking, so you stride forth with an easy gait.

Don't be upset to lose your sense of direction. The path actually doubles back and you find yourselves turned around heading north on the green trail, which actually goes nearly back to Route 25A, before returning. Part way along you can cross over on the white blaze if you prefer a shorter walk.

If everyone who walks here comes as a guest, is concerned, aware of the life preserved here, we shall have a treasured little sanctuary forever wild.

19. Hither Hills State Park

The park grounds of Hither Hills State Park cover over 1800 acres, most of it north of the Montauk Highway and little used by the campers who reserve space in the campgrounds on the Atlantic Ocean beach many months in advance. These acres offer considerable variety to the walker who will find here more miles to cover on foot than he can traverse in one day, so we have laid out an introductory walk plan for you here to allow you a look at the temptations which will make you want to come back again.

There is a large sandy arm reaching well around Napeague Harbor, and though a road will take you partially there, it is another mile on foot out to Golf Point over sandy paths, slow going, and too hot for walking in comfort in summer.

There is a stretch of three or more miles along the great curve of Napeague Bay, with pebbly underfoot, which is backed by high bluffs overlooking Block Island Sound and with good views of Gardiner's Island.

There is a lovely fresh water pond in a wooded grove which is unspoiled, and surrounded by gnarled but stunted oak trees of a venerable age.

And there are woodlands covering the hills with miles of gradual trails and, if you're as lucky as we have been, the opportunity to spot a few deer.

As you drive eastward toward Montauk the stretch of highway crosses narrow land between Napeague Harbor and the Ocean, and if you watch carefully, you'll see an obscure road which takes off directly north from the highway, crossing the RR tracks with a proper RR caution marker, and hugs the eastern shore of the Harbor. (If you come to the place the road splits with the Old Montauk Highway forking to the right and to Hither Hills Campground, then you've gone too far. Turn back!) Follow this road and park where the asphalt stops. Walk the path to your right up a gradual slope and to the top of the sand dune ahead. The vegetation

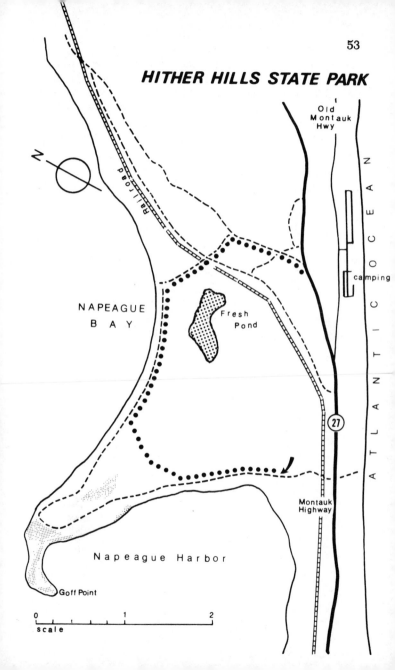

HITHER HILLS STATE PARK

Old Montauk Hwy

ATLANTIC OCEAN

N

Railroad

camping

NAPEAGUE BAY

Fresh Pond

27

Montauk Highway

Napeague Harbor

Goff Point

0   1   2
scale

is intermingled with much poison ivy. Now keep walking, north and east, down across the sands, up and over to the bay, following tracks in sand. The aspect here is reminiscent of desert and savanna. There are a couple of ponds way out on the point, too low and hidden by grasses, for you to see. The area is said to contain foxes' dens and much other wild life.

When you come to the bay, walk toward the east, and follow along the water's edge till you come to the roadway which cuts down from the bluffs. Then turn south and walk up along the road, keeping to the right, and turning on the road which takes you to the pond, where you may wish to poke around before coming out again, crossing the RR tracks and heading back. Instead of following the asphalt road, go ahead on the service road which is marked "for walkers only," and walk about 100 yards on this, then turn right and follow the dirt road back to the highway. You'll be about a mile from where you parked your car. The total distance, following this plan, will be about 5 miles.

20. Bald Hill

To suggest climbing a hill on Long Island may appear frivolous, but since we have an urge to reach heights and see the view from there, it occurs to us that others may too.

The backbone of Long Island is the Ronkonkoma moraine, starting near the Verrazano-Narrows bridge and running northeastward through roughly the middle of the island, with the highest point atop Jaynes Hill, 395 ft above sea level. West Hills Rd. will take you there, which starts off Rt. 110 near the nice old house in which Walt Whitman lived in South Huntington. West Hills Park and picnic area is on top with a trail leading the few hundred yards on to the highest point. Even on a clear day there is not much of a view. You can see a short stretch of Fire Island through a break in the trees, but that's all.

There is a fine view of Peconic Bay and Shinnecock Bay from Flanders Hill, but the new Sunrise Highway cuts right across it now and we can't suggest a good walk! Also there's a good view of Sag Harbor from Bridgehampton Race Track, but that is not a satisfactory walk either.

This leaves Bald Hill . . . which is, actually, a pleasant short walk and just may appeal to you. We've been up several times, although the path is obscure, and the first time we tried to find the path it somehow eluded us. Bald Hill is just 3 miles south of Riverhead on the west side of Route 51, the Riverhead-Moriches Road. At the junction of Wildwood lake the road jogs and slopes upward for 1.5 miles and Bald Hill is just here, not appearing to be too much above the highway.

The path in is a jeep road and, as we've said, not easily noticed. You won't have any trouble staying on the path because there are scooter tracks to the top, and you'll know when you're there all right because of the geodetic marker. The view is good in all directions. If it's clear, you should be able to see Westhampton Beach, Brookhaven Laboratory, and farm and woodlands everywhere.

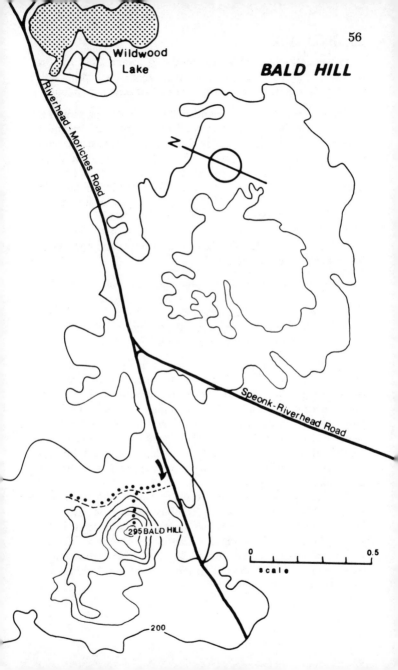

BALD HILL

Wildwood Lake

Riverhead - Moriches Road

Speonk - Riverhead Road

295 BALD HILL

200

scale
0   0.5

Woodlands are vital—they are absolutely necessary—to Long Island's future, but as in all aspects of nature, the reason for this is not obvious because of the most complex fabric which is woven around life. Woods here on Long Island are easier to get at, to cut down, to burn, than in most other places. Roots are easier to bulldoze, too, because all Long Island is just a glacial sandbar. So the speculative opportunity for profit is more so here, close to the dense centers of population, in real estate and for builders. But woodlands build soil and hold it together, act like a sponge in keeping moisture in the ground. Without water there is no life possible. Three hundred years ago the five rivers and many creeks were abundant in trout and salmon, the water level was perhaps three feet higher than today. Most of the creeks dried up as the result of the felling of the upland forest. So you see it's all tied up to the water table which has been lowering at alarming rates.

You'll find a road leading off into the woods. Extend your walk and enjoy it while you can.

21. Sears-Bellows County Park

Sears-Bellows lies to the north of the Sunrise Highway, and south of the Flanders Road, but fortunately has enough acreage to offer a feeling of remoteness, complete with two lakes, some ponds and lots of cover for deer and game birds, including the marvelously colored wood-duck. Walking here is most pleasant in spring or fall, but people are essentially gregarious, we have observed, and like to be where the crowd is, enjoy the fishing and boating at the big lake, Bellows. Thus, even when we walk here in season, a few easy strides away from the camping area and you lose almost everyone.

The best entry to the park is on a road off the Flanders Road 5 miles south of the Riverhead Traffic Circle, and a distance of less than a mile to the park entrance. There is, however, a park headquarters on the Montauk Highway about 2 miles west of Hampton Bays, and access is possible from here too.

Many service roads make good paths through the woodlands and around the lakes, and if it is a quiet day when you come, the walk around Bellows Pond is an easy one. Our favorite walk, however, is from Bellows to Sears Pond, lingering before returning. The paths are especially nice for walking, pine needles underfoot, wide and unobstructed. Go north first through woods where we always seem to put up a grouse or two, past a pond on the right which is a favorite haunt of the wood-duck, then swing to the left and into a clearing which has a significant rise of land on it. We usually climb the rise and sit for a few minutes because there often seems to be a red-tailed hawk here circling, and there is a view of the surrounding country. We rejoin the path on the other side of the hill and walk about a mile northwestward through sparse, burned over, woods. The growth and vegetation increases heavily as you come to Sears Pond. Go down to the water quietly, the ducks are wary in this secluded hideaway. Across the pond you will see two osprey nests, one in disrepair, the other has been

SEARS-BELLOWS COUNTY PARK

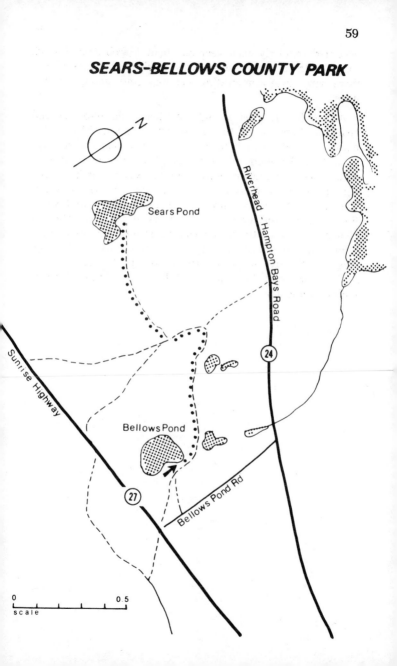

occupied regularly each year on about March 21st through summer. If you have the patience to sit in the duck blinds, there are always interesting comings and goings on the water.

Although it is quiet enough to listen to the birdsong, and hear the flapping of the ducks wing, the muffled traffic noises from the two highways do carry across the treetops as well as jetsounds of overhead planes on their route to New York and punctuations from monstrous earth moving equipment or chainsaws which carry into this quiet world. This is true, of course, anyplace on Long Island, and Sears-Bellows is as free today of the sounds of our civilization as almost anywhere else. So we can be grateful for the relative calm and tranquility and hope that others, too, will recognize it and strive to perpetuate it. And be thankful for the settings provided for public use by a foresighted County Park Commission.

The Peconic river runs west to east and, where it pours out into Flanders Bay, Riverhead hugs its northern banks. Just below Riverhead, two four-lane highways radiate more or less from the Riverhead traffic circle which borders on a large pie-shaped section of wild land. One of these roads is the new road to Calverton, which parallels the river on the south; the other is Route 51, swinging around the Suffolk County Government Center, and southwesterly toward Moriches. This wild area has two distinctly different habitats, one of the few remaining cedar swamps of once extensive freshwater wetlands on Long Island, and an inland pine barren, where pitch pine is the dominant cover. We enjoy good walks in both habitats.

The cedar swamp is undeveloped county park land with a sign, *Cranberry Bog*, relatively easy to locate. The asphalt road to Wildwood Lake one mile south from the Riverhead Circle displays the sign on your right, just after Lakeside Drive, which veers off to the left. Although the park is usually closed, there are a few unmarked trails and it is a place which makes a fascinating ramble. You can't really walk around Sweezy Pond because it is much too swampy to the northwest, however good firm ground takes you into the pond by a service road and you can stay on the solid paths and walk around at least half of it. The old cranberry fields lie to the east of the pond, and dikes permit you to penetrate some of the jungly growth so you feel you should be able to join the highway beyond. We say it is a ramble because to enjoy this spot is to explore, walking here and there along fringes of the wetlands. But we implore you: walk quietly and cautiously, respecting stillness and wildlife. Deer and heron, swan and geese as well as duck live here, so try especially hard not to disturb. The variety of shrub and ground cover is extraordinary—sweet pepperbush, bayberry, beach plumb, wild grape, bearberry, cranberry, bear oak, so many bog plants, and the pond is full of waterlilies, slender arrowhead and reed—a catalogue of freshwater swamplands

CRANBERRY BOG

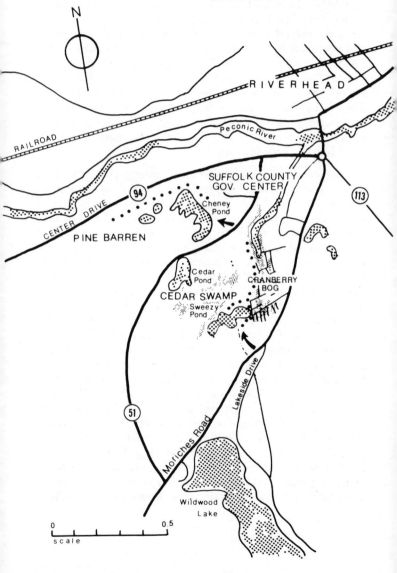

N

RIVERHEAD

RAILROAD

Peconic River

CENTER DRIVE

94

Cheney Pond

SUFFOLK COUNTY GOV. CENTER

113

PINE BARREN

Cedar Pond

CEDAR SWAMP

CRANBERRY BOG

Sweezy Pond

51

Lakeside Drive

Moriches Road

Wildwood Lake

0   0.5

scale

growth. If you like this kind of exploring you should enjoy this. The walking will cover probably two miles, but take a couple of hours.

As for the pine barrens, park to the southeast of Suffolk County Government Center and walk in on one of the dirt service roads, west off the Moriches Road. Fire doesn't destroy a pitch pine forest, which lives to sprout again, and although it used to be commercially exploited for resins and fuel, it no longer is. It is greedy for light and can be snuffed out when shaded by oak.

Location of Short Walks on Long Island

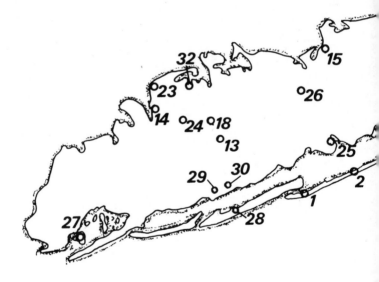

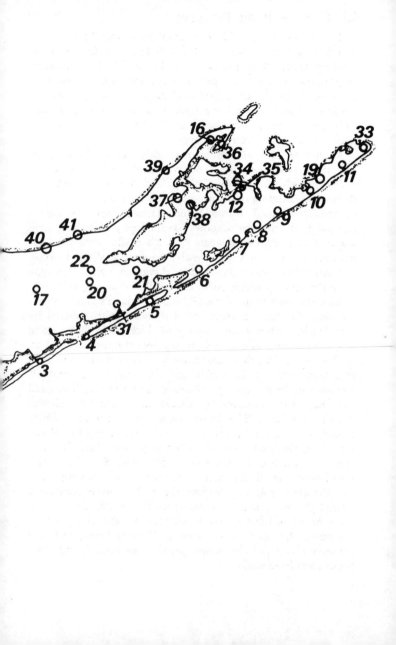

The Nassau County Museum administers this 72 acre area, which is a former estate and which has over five miles of walking trails. Although it is in the midst of a suburban neighborhood, it has unexpected riches and points of interest. Turn north off the Long Island Expressway, or off Northern Boulevard, on to Glen Cove Road and follow it until it runs right into Garvies Point Road, at the end of which lies the land in the Garvies Point Preserve.

A parking area adjoins a great little museum containing a working archeological laboratory, and the exhibits give you a fine introduction to the Long Island before its European discovery. Standing in the museum you have a sweeping view of the Hempstead Harbor. And starting here are eleven marked trails over the roughly V-shaped plot, providing good walking at any time of year. And it's easily accessible, has unusual variety; so walk silently, keeping a sharp lookout, and you have more interesting things in store than you would imagine possible on an old family estate like this.

Like the high ridge along all of Long Island's North Shore, the shoreline here is made up of morainal hills covered by woodlands, with a heavy canopy in thickets. Walking along the outer trails you'll be able to see over the tops of trees on to the Sound. Out there are many species of ducks, and gulls and terns. During the spring and fall migrations, warblers are seen in trees close by. Walking inland toward the pond you may see pheasants, grosbeaks and cardinals. Hermit thrush nest here. The fresh water pond attracts rabbits, raccoons, turtles and frogs—even an occasional red fox. Walking along the trail down the front slope look into the open meadow, which is an attractive feeding ground to other wildlife—insects, small mammals and birds. And walking along the shoreline you can inspect the rocky beach containing glacial debris so characteristic of all the North Shore. Only a few spots on Long Island, however, have glacial deposits so unusually thin as they are here at Garvies Point, and well preserved fossils of Cretaceous plants have been found along these shorefront cliffs.

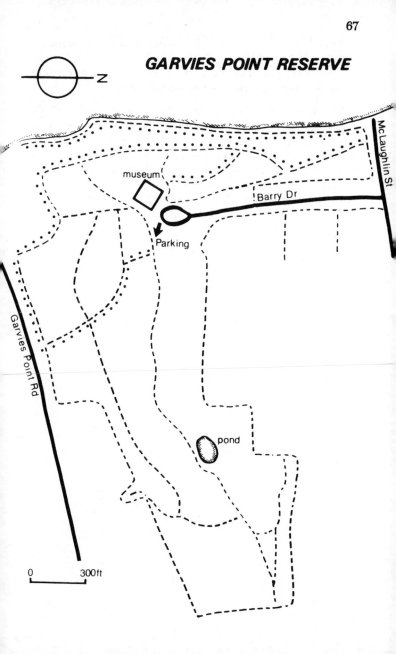

GARVIES POINT RESERVE

museum

Barry Dr

Parking

Garvies Point Rd

McLaughlin St

pond

0   300ft

There's an effort to keep the whole preserve in a natural state, and it provides a wide variety of native plants. Northern red oak, pine oak, sassafras, beech, black cherry, tulip trees and, in damp areas, red maples and tupelos.

The Matinecock Indians were the tribe who roamed the woodlands east of Cold Spring Harbor and had an encampment here on this hill when the English settlers first arrived. They had made use of it for hundreds of years. Shellfish, taken from the Sound, were baked at their campsites and collected in mounds. And pottery fragments, as well as arrowheads, uncovered here show that primitive life had been sustained here far earlier, and can be traced as far as 3000 BC.

Just about anybody would acknowledge that John S. Phipps and wife had the wherewithal to enjoy, and that they understood the art of, gracious living. They grew their own almost everything. Besides a swimming pool, a private golf course, both indoor and outdoor tennis courts, they had two of their own polo fields! Moreover, they had the 18th century Georgian style house, and gardens to go with it, with appropriate furnishings throughout.

Almost no one can afford to live this way anymore, but it is fun to imagine. And if you enjoy snooping through other people's houses, and walking like the Sun King around tended grounds, then Old Westbury Gardens is definitely a place for you. We have included it in these walks on Long Island because we loved it, and friends of ours who live nearby, rave about it and come back again and again.

Take the Guinea Woods South exit off the LI Expressway. East on the service road 1.2 miles. Right on Old Westbury Road ¼ mile. Admission to the gardens and house is $2.50 for adults. You should allow two hours, and be sure to do everything including a walk around the lake, and a visit to see the animals—some adorable minature Argentinian horses and Mediterranean donkeys.

You enter through wrought iron gates, the grass is tended, and you will not believe the beech and linden trees which immediately establish an important theme.

The place is consciously full of surprises. For example, when you come into the house, there are fresh flowers in all rooms, the dinner table is set; it is just as though the Phipps family had stepped out but would be back shortly, that you were an invited weekend guest. The rooms are pleasant: light, airy, homey. And someone with a fine sense of color has decorated it tastefully. It is not ostentatious, but it is a display of considerable wealth.

Out of doors has everything, and everywhere there is delight in the unexpected, theatrical sense to the gardens,

OLD WESTBURY GARDENS

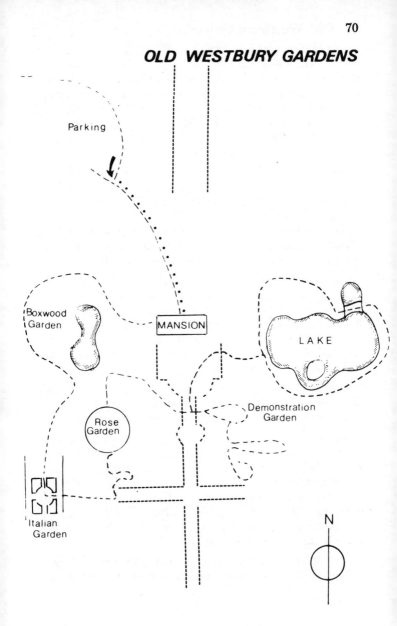

looking down on the boxwood garden, coming upon the Italian, discovering the Pinetum. And allees are magnificent!

Now all this is arranged with a self-guided tour and map, so you will have a fine walk of it. Although you quickly get lost—we suspect that it was planned this way. Besides, there are discreet signs which tell you where you are, and how to keep going to where you should.

For anyone with a plot of ground and a yearning to husband it, the demonstration gardens alone are worth the admission. Our suggestion is to bring along a pencil and pad to make notes.

We were happy because rabbits, chipmunks and a black capped chickadee seemed to welcome us!

Anyone familiar with Central Park knows the genius of Frederick Law Olmsted in grouping trees together. See what he started here on the banks of the Connetquot River on a very rich man's estate in 1887. There are 690 acres with trim lawns and open meadows, a wild flower garden, a marshy refuge, and paths lead everywhere. Along the river's edge, around and through woods, it is difficult to imagine a nicer walk anywhere that has a setting more gracious than the one provided for public use here. The estate is maintained by the Long Island State Park and Recreation Commission, given in trust to the state by Mr. Cutting's daughter, though it is not technically a State Park. There is no picnicking. Open daily. An admission of 75¢ is made for adults. To reach the arboretum turn east off the end of the Southern State Parkway just before it reaches Heckscher, and follow carefully marked signs.

There are five different trails laid out and marked, each with different colors, and were you to take the allotted time on each, the total time suggested would be 3½ hours. We recommend that you plan to spend at least 2½ hours here, and make a most pleasant morning or afternoon of it by combining two or more of these walks into one longer one.

There is also a seasonal aspect to consider in planning your walk here. Wildflowers should be out in late March and April, rhododendrons in late May and June. Changing colors are engaging of course, and chrysanthemums may intrigue you into coming early in October. Even on a hot summer's day, however, the welcome release is here, a cooling breeze off the river, shade from the mature trees, and benches conveniently at hand will probably quietly lure you to sit a spell.

The rambly old informal house is maintained in good repair, and partially open. Tea and simple snacks are available cafeteria style, and tables on the large enclosed porch

BAYARD CUTTING ARBORETUM

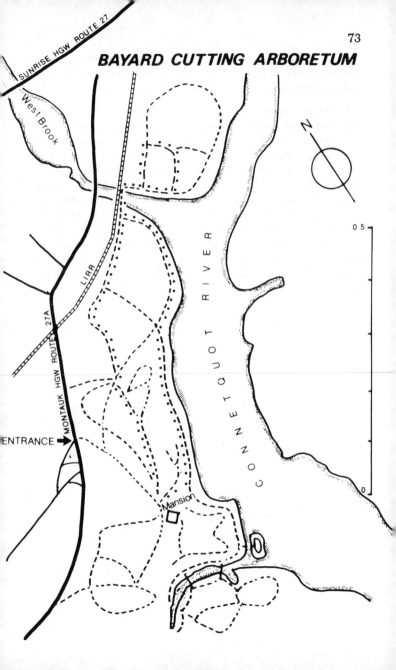

looking out over the river offer an attractive setting for a relaxing break. A fine collection of stuffed birds is on display and should be recommended too to visitors.

Heckscher State Park does not offer much in the way of discovery, and so we wouldn't especially recommend it to a serious walker. But because it adjoins the Cutting estate it does call for comment. There are 1700 acres and it is easy to get off alone in the woods, away from the vast picnic and playfield areas. It should offer more solitude during times when these fields are not so heavily used as they are in summer. An old dirt service road leads to the northwest corner, down along the west boundary and out to parking area #5, reserved as a small boat ramp. In early spring you may find it more interesting. Generally, it is a scrub oak woods with marshy places, and you should find wild flowers then.

26. Blydenburgh County Park

East of Old Willets Pass the large former Weld Estate of over 600 acres is open now to the public as Blydenburgh, a Suffolk County Park. It is woodland with swamps and fields, and with Stump Pond, which we understand is second in size on Long Island only to Lake Ronkonkoma. The lake is long and irregularly shaped, somewhat like a boot with a long pointed toe. No swimming is permitted here, but there are row boats available, and so it is a popular fishing place as well as camp ground. Several trails, or dirt roads, make for easy walking, and there is some horseback riding.

The best way to get there is from the western edge of Smithtown Branch on Route 25, the Jericho turnpike. Turn south off the turnpike at the traffic signal on Brookside Drive and go one block. Then west on New Mill Road which leads directly into the park. You will find parking space here, as in all Suffolk County Parks, limited to Suffolk County residents with permits. Trails are not heavy traffic areas, and hikers are not discouraged. Rangers are very nice fellows generally, and if you do not have the permit will usually treat you courteously if you yourselves are not a nuisance.

Our suggestion on a good walk here is to follow the trail from the house by the parking area down to Stump Pond. The trees near the house have all been planted, but are native to the area. Once all this was tended farmland, but it was allowed sometime ago to go back to nature. Now plants and surrounding shore are slowly filling in the lake, and everywhere is becoming overgrown. The area covered by the lake is 120 acres, and the fish consist of bass, sunfish, bluegills as well as a few trout. The plants are common water lily and yellow pond lily, as well as water milfoil. You continue on the path southward across the bridge by the mill, and along the western shores of the lake to the stream which you follow until the trail splits. Take the one to your left, which crosses the stream, goes up the hill and then follow it back so that you reach the high bluff of the peninsula from which you see a whole panorama of the lake. The

BLYDENBURGH COUNTY PARK

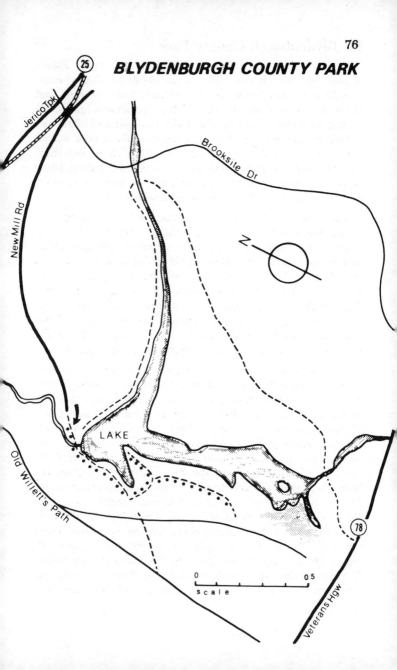

25

Jerico Tpk

New Mill Rd

Brooksite Dr

N

LAKE

Old Willett's Path

78

0   0.5
scale

Veterans Hgw

walk to this point is little over a mile, and if you wish to extend it you can continue along the fire road to the southern reaches of the lake, though it is much too marshy on this south end to continue on around. Another plan is to return to the mill, then walk eastward about a mile along the northern shore, crossing the toe at the extreme end, and follow the path westerly as far as you wish. As you will discover, there is considerable variety in the plant and animal life and we think you'll have a good outing here. In the fall you may see Eastern bluebird, cedar waxwing and brown creeper in these woods.

27. Jamaica Bay Wildlife Refuge

The sun sets in a splash of pinkish mauve behind the towers of the city. A jumbo jet floats silently into Kennedy on the other side of the bay. And West Pond at Jamaica Bay's Wildlife Refuge is alive, teeming with swooping terns, black skimmers seining their dinners through their amazing red bills, plovers and phalaropes skittering about in the shallows, the great white and blue heron standing, majestic, in the tall reeds. This is late afternoon in early August. The juxtaposition here of what man hath wrought in the distance with the magnificence of nature in the foreground, calls attention strikingly to whether we can keep a balance between these sometimes inimical forces.

You need a permit to visit the refuge, easily obtainable from the New York City Department of Parks, 830 Fifth Avenue, NYC 10021. If you care to drive (Belt Parkway then turn south or Cross Bay Blvd.) there is a parking lot on the westside of Cross Bay Blvd. 1.4 miles south of the first bridge. Look for one discreet sign. Or you can come by subway. The IND Far Rockaway A or E train takes you there for 70¢ (Broad Channel Exit). In case you do, you walk back one mile to the entrance. But don't be put off by a series of shack dwellings cheek by jowl on the edges of the bay, sitting upon tenuous foundations. This walk is incidental.

The refuge itself comprises 18 2/3 square miles, much of it islands and tidal marshes. The accessible spot is the West Pond region, and West Pond is a 20 acre fresh water pond. A first trip to the Jamaica Bay Refuge is inspiring, especially undertaken at sunrise or sunset. Those responsible for seeing the possibilities, creating here a forever wild area available to birds on the Atlantic flyway, and people via the subway, deserve highest praise and homage. Sit on one of the benches and turn your glasses or scope on these creatures. Many will use Jamaica Bay as a regular stop-over during spring or fall migrations. Maybe as you sit here the short eared owl will rise from the grasses and swoop about

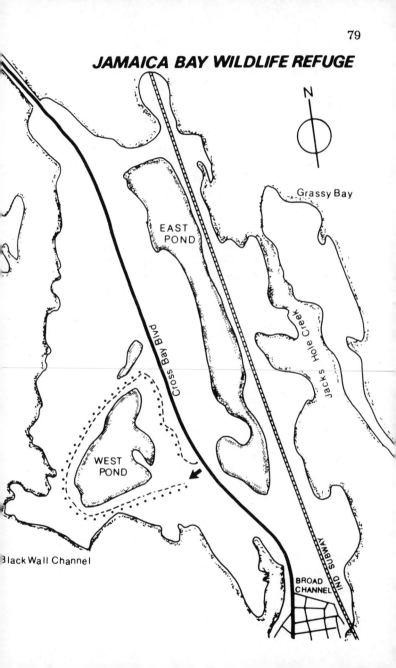

JAMAICA BAY WILDLIFE REFUGE

on his nocturnal search for a mouse or two. Even if you don't know one bird from another the whole setting will impress you.

There are a few suggestions we'd make after urging you to stop in or write for a permit. Bring along your bird book and, if it's a buggy time of year, your favorite insect repellent. Although there's usually a breeze and they may not bother you, in some grassy protected areas, you may wish you had brought it along. Also, eat before you come. No picnicking is allowed, and there is no place to dine nearby.

Across on the east side of the road there is another larger section of the Refuge with a 100 acre pond and shoreline on the bay as well. Sometimes rare birds stop here, and you may want to look in, if you have strength after your walk around West Pond—almost 2 miles. If so, look in from the northwest.

28. John F. Kennedy Memorial Wildlife Sanctuary

As you fly into Kennedy Airport you realize that the surrounding area is a vast network of tidal marshes, low lying islands like lilypads in the bay, and barrier beaches conspicuously uninhabited by man, which cause us to speculate on wildlife there. Knowing that the sea rising over a marsh floods this land with chemical riches, that tides moderate temperatures here, and that wildlife in wetlands is abundant, we are intrigued by the thousands of acres behind Jones Beach. So if you speculate about this as we do, then we must recommend to you the John F. Kennedy Memorial Wildlife Sanctuary.

It is a 500 acre stretch, swallowed up by over 5000 acres owned by Oyster Bay Town and managed by the New York State Conservation Department, but provides an opportunity to investigate something of what wetlands life is about. You must obtain a permit to visit the Sanctuary by writing to the Superintendent of Beaches, Town of Oyster Bay. Drive through the Tobay Beach parking lot (just east of parking area #9) and into the parking place provided within the sanctuary itself.

There is an old road, just about a mile long, which leads through the middle of the area and provides good footing, although absolutely flat and unspectacular because it is bordered by plants growing to a height just over your head, the usual variety of beach and swamp growth. You can leave the road in several places and walk to blinds, or to the observation tower from which you can sweep your glasses over the pond and the tree tops, but you cannot get much closer on foot to the water.

It was after Labor Day when we walked here, spent a longer time and walked farther than we intended, and were exhausted. From the tower we had watched a large brown female marsh hawk for sometime quartering low over the marshes, its white rump patch marking distinctly visible, its

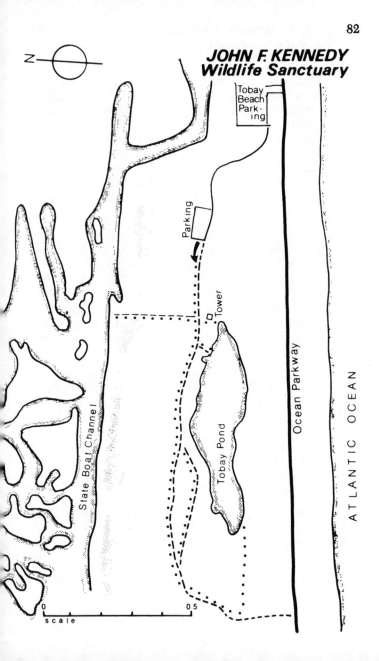

N

JOHN F. KENNEDY
Wildlife Sanctuary

Tobay
Beach
Parking

Parking

Tower

State Boat Channel

Tobay Pond

Ocean Parkway

ATLANTIC OCEAN

0   0.5
scale

buoyant, tilting glide a joy to observe. There were clouds of tree swallows swooping about, and low cherry trees alive with cedar waxwings. We thought we saw a prothonotary warbler. Glossy ibis flew purposefully overhead. Duck arrived at the pond, skidding in for a landing. Kingbirds and white egrets were common, heron and belted kingfishers scarce.

The black and orange monarch butterfly were assembled in spectacular concentrations. These frail insects are notorious for the long treks they make on their annual mass migrations, and all morning continuously called attention to their flutterings.

Bayberry bushes were heavy with fruit, catbriar was in tangles. We noticed that birds had eaten the berries from the pokeweed. When we stretched out to rest on the white sandy dunes which overlook the pond from the northwest, we looked up at a sky everywhere interrupted by winged creatures.

29. Tackapusha Preserve

Access to the Tackapusha Preserve, just south of the Sunrise Highway in the Village of Seaford, is easy. Turn south on Washington Avenue, go four or five short blocks, and you'll see the Museum to the East, and alongside, a parking lot.

This little building is a division of the Nassau County Museum of Natural History, and well worth a visit. Inside are informative displays, literature, and usually a nature film to see; and behind there's a small menagerie with Long Island wildlife, allowing you a good close look at an American bittern, for instance.

Surprising is the preserve itself, which maintains 80 acres in the midst of all suburbia. Divided into three sections—the southern area can be entered just to the North of the parking area, and a trail goes up alongside the Seaford Creek, crosses and returns down the other; in all a half hour or so walk. Because the stream meanders and branches there are lots of marshy areas within the main body of the stream, and on the sides are taller trees. It is a good stroll for a spring or autumn day and in no way strenuous. You'll see white oak, red maple and one of the very few remaining stands of Atlantic white cedar on Long Island. There are shadbush, spicebush, pepperbush, and high blueberry. On the ground, fern, and in spring, flowers—wood anemone and pink lady's slipper.

Because of the variety of plants and insects there are many different birds at any time of year. A pamphlet listing nearly 200 different species and times of year when you might expect to see them is available at the Museum.

There are two other areas besides this north of the Sunrise Highway, which are restricted to limited access for special purposes, as the intent is to preserve the areas and keep them as wild as possible. There are paths around both. The northernmost section is better drained, drier and has open grassy areas. The middle section has a small pond. If you're interested, inquire at the Museum.

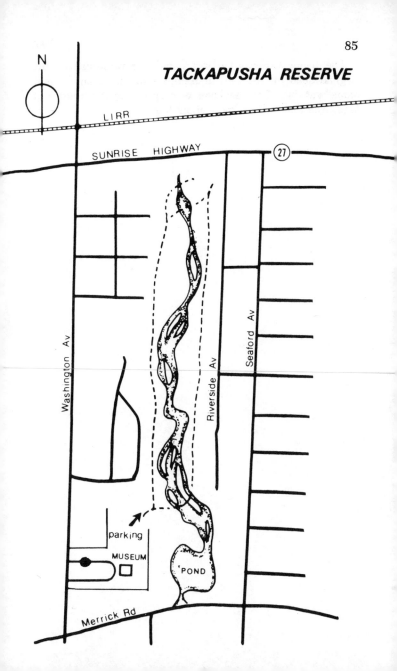

TACKAPUSHA RESERVE

The name Tackapusha, incidentally, is preserved on the original deed for the land in Hempstead. An Indian by that name was one of the sachems who agreed to the transfer of land. And that's all we know about him.

A quiet place in the midst of superhighways and dense population, but a pleasant walk of a couple of miles up and back. A crystal clear stream flowed freshly when we walked here, some kids fished at one of the dams and two boys had a little rubber raft in the stream. The Massapequa Preserve is a wooded strip, drained by a stream dammed in a couple of places, thus making rather weedy ponds, excellent cover for ducks. The walking is chiefly along a dirt road (no cars) which runs along the stream, although there are paths into the woods and around ponds. In August the fragrance of sweet pepper bush permeated the air. We watched a least tern hover and dip over a pond, slamming into the water to capture a tiny minnow, and a family of black ducks float secretively through the reeds. Deep rose petals of the rose-mallow flowers, with their bright yellow centers, made a handsome display along the edge of the stream.

The quiet strip on which to walk is all north of Clark Blvd., and it is possible to park nearby on Lake Shore Drive, which runs on the east; or Parkside Blvd., which runs on the west of the preserve. There is an entrance through the fence on Clark Blvd. It is also a short walk from Massapequa Park RR Station.

There are several parks or preserves in Nassau county with similar characteristics, long and narrow in shape and including a stream and a pond or two, not the sort of property that developers look for. They provide drainage and some wetlands and are set aside as green space. That much at least the ecologists and nature enthusiasts have been able to get across. And they really are an asset. It's another matter, however, when it comes to taking care of this precious greenery. Preserves or parks are beautifully kept only where civic pride is a reality. For the most part our senses have not been awakened to the terrible affront the carelessly tossed bit of plastic or, most blatantly, the beer can, represents.

MASSAPEQUA PRESERVE

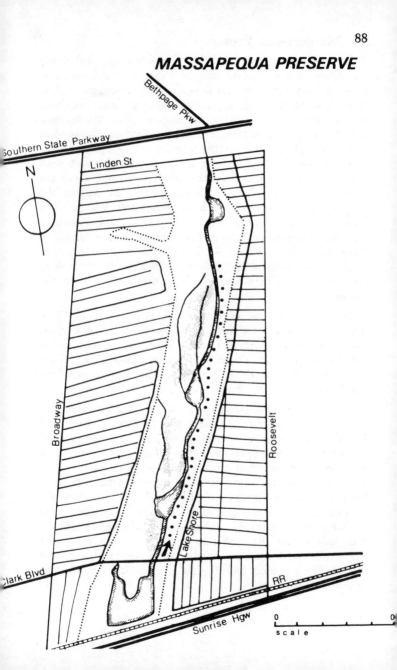

As we walk through the sweet smelling lane in the Massapequa Preserve we wondered why it was so carelessly regarded, why so many beer cans had been left behind, why we have failed to instill awareness in our children. What happened to the Boy or Girl Scouts who scoured this area? Where is the point of pride to keep it beautiful? Do sheer numbers of people living closely together necessarily obliterate everyone's sensitivity? Will communities carelessly ignore the fragrant sweet pepperbush and the dainty bright orange jewel weed and all other plants and flowers that can make a Massapequa preserve an oasis only if respected? How long can we ignore the careless habit of litter anywhere?

This walk along the stream can be a delightful surprise, however, and we recommend it. If you wish, you may extend it further by following the footpath along the east side of the Bethpage State Parkway, which begins here and runs right to Bethpage State Park (about 1.5 miles).

31. The Quogue Sanctuary

Citizens of Quogue set aside roughly 1500 acres of wetlands, Upper Quantuck Bay, ponds and woodland, for a refuge for birds and for plant life which have good trails and make for a pleasant short walk. The details of the way the place has developed suggest a talented and dedicated professional guidance. The sanctuary lies just north of the RR tracks above the Village of Quogue on Scrub Oak Road, which runs north from the Montauk Highway and makes its way around into the Quogue-Riverhead Road.

As you come into the preserve there is a nice small zoo—a talking crow welcomes you, and there are other examples of local animals. Nearby, in a fenced area, are some deer. And wild turkey roam at will in the open foraging area. There is also a small aviary of rare tropical birds and several tall martin houses. The large pond just at the entrance has a permanent resident fleet of Canada geese, and varieties of ducks and waterfowl seasonally.

In spring Canada geese families go about training their young, parading in the grass, one parent ahead and one behind, and the little flock between. Somehow they find the living so good here they stay.

Walking is clear cut. You can take the path that goes around the pond, or the one that follows the perimeter. We often decide to do both. Wherever you go you will see typical flora of the Long Island uplands, oak and pine interspersed with various berry bushes birds like to feed on. The ground cover is bearberry and blueberry, and there is black cherry, beach plum and shadbush, as well as nearly 70 varieties of wild flowers. One summer we were delighted to find in a boggy spot, a small stand of the exquisite tiny white blossomed bog orchid.

There are a number of places to sit and quietly observe, whichever path you take. Very often, on the ice pond to the north, there'll be a little green heron or some mallards. You can explore this refuge with no fear of getting lost.

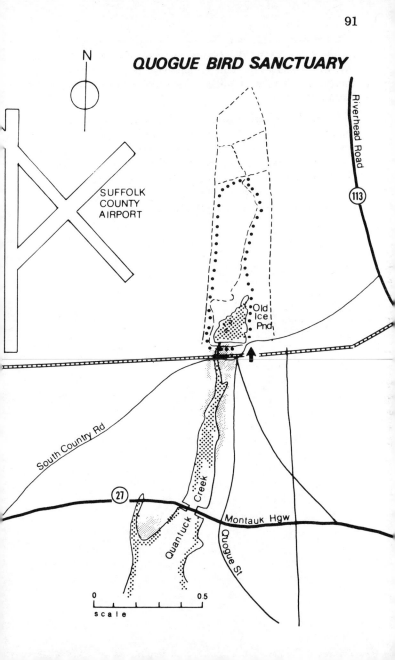

QUOGUE BIRD SANCTUARY

Once you swing all the way around and return on the southern shores of the big pond, you cross a swale on an extensive boardwalk where, amongst fern and tree roots, there are apt to be families of mallards, and assorted lively birds in the trees.

All in all a pleasant place to walk, in no way taxing, worth the leisurely pace so that you can use your field glasses. The acreage abuts the inactive Suffolk County Air Force base so it seems even more spacious. And the average visitor with children looks at the animals in the zoo and doesn't venture much beyond the edge of the pond, therefore paths are relatively little used, making it pleasant walking.

32. North Shore Bird and Game Sanctuary
   in Mill Neck

Native trees and jungly growth on Barbados was all cut down many years ago to make way for neat fields of sugar cane. In Welchman's Hall Gully on that tropical island however, there is a wonderland through which a visitor can stroll because this gully has little commercial value and the native growth remains. So it is in the sanctuary at Mill Neck, a ravine with little commercial value that has become sacrosanct by marvelous good fortune, that has been set aside as a preserve by generous minded and farsighted donors. All around it in this old community are large estates which for many years have been kept up beautifully, and beside the natural protection the sanctuary gets from its setting, it is reinforced by being completely fenced in. Hence this is a protected area especially favored, a lovely place to walk, a wet woodland and along a marshy estuary, which is filled with birds and magnificent trees.

Although open dawn to dusk, we recommend that you let them know you are coming, because the only parking (no parking along any roads in Mill Neck) is in a place provided within, and if the gate is locked you're out of luck! And you can do this by writing ahead. To reach the parking area turn north off Route 25A, on Wolver Hollow Road, follow it until it runs into Chicken Valley Road continuing on north on it to Oyster Bay Road. Turn right to Mill Road, which continues north to the Long Island RR tracks crossing, a viaduct over Mill Road. The sanctuary is just here to the south of the tracks, and west of Mill Road. Incidentally, it is just a short walk from the Mill Neck RR station.

We are prompted to write a few words about the tuliptree, because the magnificent stand of tuliptrees here along estuarial waters is inspiring, towering as they do probably one hundred feet high, their trunks tall and straight and branchless for the first fifty or sixty feet.Considered the handsomest eastern forest tree because of its upright trunk and perfect symmetry, the tuliptree is frequently seen as an ornamental,

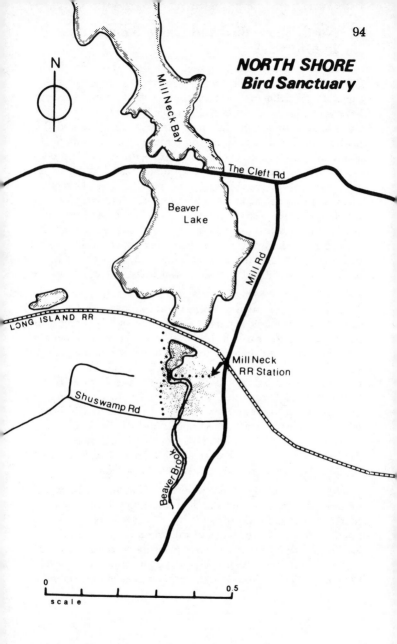

N

**NORTH SHORE
Bird Sanctuary**

Mill Neck Bay

The Cleft Rd

Beaver
Lake

Mill Rd

LONG ISLAND RR

Mill Neck
RR Station

Shuswamp Rd

Beaver Brook

0   0.5
scale

and is scattered throughout Long Island. However, the stand here is rare, perhaps unique, in numbers of trees well over 150 years old. Their old bark is rich brown, deeply fissured, and some must have diameters of four feet or more. Another name by which this tree is known is canoetree, because Indians made their dugouts from them, and when the English settlers first arrived they found Indians travelling all about Long Island in them. Surrounded by these ancient trees, looking up at those towering trunks, you may see how this was possible—though without tools it took great ingenuity and patience, skill with fire and endless hours to fashion a seagoing craft of one. These trees give you reason to gasp and to consider the wonder of it all.

33. Montauk State Park

A spacious parking lot 132 miles from New York City at the end of the Montauk Highway in the Montauk State Park and the weekend specials to Montauk the Long Island Railway runs, attest to the popularity of this place. But the attraction which brings the crowds should not dissuade you as a walker. Choose your time, and move away from crowds. Montauk is an experience, and you are apt to enjoy it if you are a loner and nature lover. There's a raw bleakness here: hills of shadbush and bayberry, almost endless dunes, and an incessant surf chewing away at the bolders, tumbling stones that cackle in a noisy babble. We've come here at dawn, before the sun was up, at least twice, and will come again. If you come at this hour you won't be alone. Surf fishermen will be here before you. You can walk for miles in either direction. We've been here at midday, and at sunset too, lingering afterwards in the twilight. So, although it is wiser to rhapsodize about winter, spring or fall, our experience is that there's something for you in any season at any hour of day in Montauk.

Where to go? As you leave the parking area follow the path north of the lighthouse down into the gully to the little pond. Wild flowers, birds of the thicket and pond life are here. Then cross over the dunes on to the beach and walk south to the point. If you're here at low tide you can walk as far as you are able. The other direction northwest along the beach fronting Block Island Sound is a less crowded walk, the farther you go the fewer people, and the more abundant the shore birds. Montauk is a birding area; come equipped with field glasses. There's a handsome new heavy-timbered, glassy refreshment building which serves sandwiches, snacks and coffee, but if you're interested in food, bring your own.

The Montauk State Park covers 724 acres so if you only walk those beaches easily accessible from the main parking area, you have not done justice in exploring it. On the way out you'll see dirt roads off to your right. Parking here and

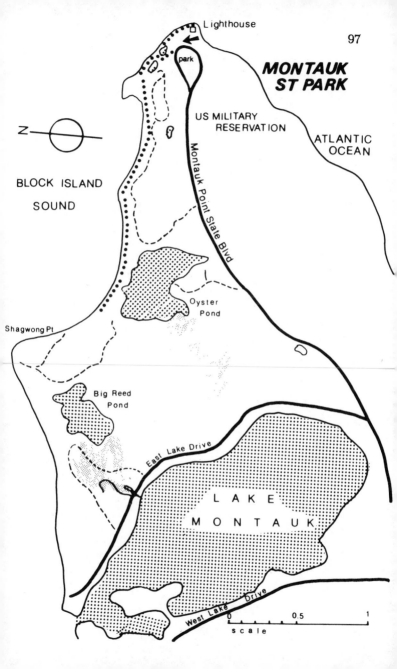

Lighthouse

park

MONTAUK ST PARK

US MILITARY
RESERVATION

ATLANTIC
OCEAN

N

BLOCK ISLAND

SOUND

Montauk Point State Blvd

Shagwong Pt

Oyster
Pond

Big Reed
Pond

East Lake Drive

L A K E

M O N T A U K

West Lake Drive

0   0.5   1
s c a l e

walking down one through the woods is pleasant, and search-ing for the short eared owl will take you to Oyster Pond. Or another plan is to drive north off the highway on East Lake Drive, continuing on beyond the lake and the airport to your right, to one of the parking places at the very end of the road. From here you can cross the beach and walk eastward toward Shagwong Point, and beyond to the Park.

From the bluffs on the point, during the fall migration period, it is not unusual to see the jaegers, petrels, phalaropes and other species which usually are seen only far out to sea.

In the town of Easthampton, 6.5 miles directly north of Georgica, occupying one of the many peninsulas which jut into the waters surrounding Eastern Long Island and give this area such meandering shapes, is Cedar Point, a choice County Park of 600 acres.

To find the park entrance, turn at Georgica off the Montauk Highway (Route 27) on Stephen Hands Path and follow it north to the Old Northwest Road, continuing on to the crossing of Alewife Brook Road. The Park is there to the north. Or, driving from Easthampton, follow Three Mile Harbor Road and turn left on Springy Banks Road, which also runs into the Alewife Brook Road.

You enter the Northwest Woods, a high bluff generally 50 feet above the waters of Gardiner's Bay to the north, and drop down alongside Alewife Pond to Cedar Pond beyond where you'll find a camping and parking area. There are deer in these woods, look sharply in the late afternoon. When you park you can walk out on the spit which points west. It's a fine walk. And though surely you may temporarily lose your sense of direction, you'll look south on to Northwest Harbor and Barcelona Point, west on to Shelter Island, northwest on to Orient Beach State Park and northeast on to Gardiner's Island, but eventually the geography of these fingers and watery shores will sort themselves out.

The walk to the point is just over a mile. The inner shore sandy, the outer one pebbly. Or, from this entry east along a stretch of wild beach to Lafarges Landing is a distance of two miles. Whichever way you choose to go, or both, will be delightful, particularly in early spring or fall—summer afternoons can be crowded. Jingle shells, scallop shells, boatshells or slipper shells, and pear shaped whelks are nature's handiworks you'll find here, along with all the other flotsam which give beachcombing variety.

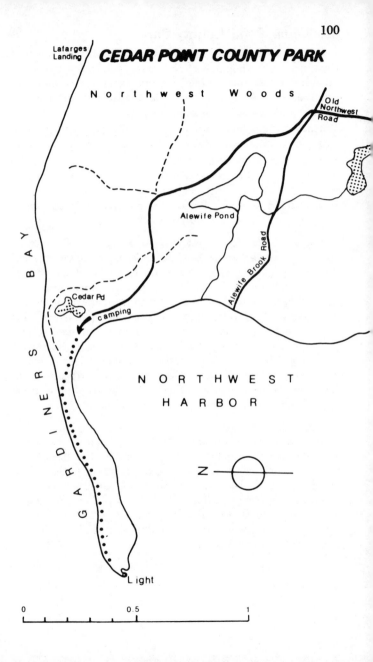

CEDAR POINT COUNTY PARK

Northwest Creek spreads out into an ample harbor, offering a secluded mooring for small boats and is a prime Long Island wetland, now protected by the county. You drive on to a large parking area near the harbor with the shore beyond. On the left the creek fingers deep into a marsh. When we first came upon this out-of-the-way place, a lady came up to us as we were looking through our field glasses, and asked if we had seen her ospreys. It was early April, and she said they were back again, pointing to a tree on the border of the wood at the edge of the marsh, and saying that their nest had been knocked off the platform, but that she was hoping they would build again soon. At that time we had never had a close look at one of these magnificent hawks, so we shared her excitement. Since then the ban on DDT has been invoked and many of us hope osprey will breed again successfully on Long Island.

The ambience of Northwest Creek is wonderfully wild. And the spit of land which reaches around the harbor is a beautiful place to walk. Because of what is underfoot it sets you thinking about primeval beginnings. In stacks of dried sea grasses are carapaces of many horseshoe crabs, the tiniest not much bigger than your thumb, left behind by moulting crab. Actually the horseshoe is not a crab at all but of the same family as the spider, a living fossil whose relatives became extinct 400 million years ago. Then the fiddler crab burrows here in the moist sand among the reeds. Neat little balls of sand piled meticulously beside his burrow look as though he had a machine to turn them out exactly calibrated. At low tide it is clear that the salt marsh is groaning with an abundant nourishment for birds and fish.

There is really no particular path to follow to the bay here, step wherever you can. An old pair of sneakers is the best footgear because, although damp, it isn't necessary to wade. The beach proper is narrow with an array of scallop shells which sea gulls drop. Often the whole operation is so neat that the two parts of the shell are still together after the gull has extracted his dinner. At the east end the beach is

NORTHWEST CREEK

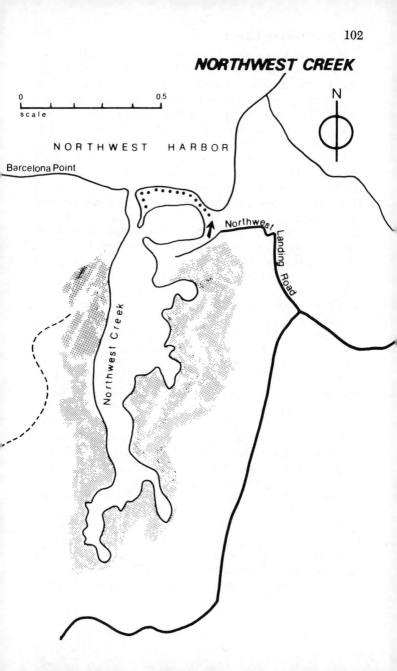

NORTHWEST HARBOR

Barcelona Point

Northwest Landing Road

Northwest Creek

N

0   0.5
scale

low with tidal pools, but as you walk westward toward the inlet and Barcelona Point, the dunes get higher, perhaps put there when they dredged the inlet after a storm. You can walk all the way around the edge of the beach and back to the little harbor, making an elongated circle of perhaps a couple of miles. Most people who come here are on boats and don't comb the beach. It is relatively an undisturbed treasure trove of the things Rachel Carson talks about so eloquently in her book "The Edge of the Sea."

To get to Northwest Creek, turn north on Stephen Hands Path at Georgica, then follow Northwest Road to the very end. It twists and turns, goes through miles of pine, and you hope that it will stay this way for a long time.

36. Orient Beach State Park

At the end of Route 24 on the north fork of Long Island, just before you get to the water and the ferry to New London, on your right is the usual rustic state park sign for Orient Beach—but Orient Beach is not a usual state park. Turn and drive along the causeway to the parking lot. If it's spring or early summer, look to your right as you go along the causeway for the osprey nest across the water. A faithful pair returns yearly, and they are magnificent birds, these fish hawk. Sometimes you can watch them fish, diving from on high as they glide past, and catching a fish as much as 10 feet below the surface with their talons.

There is a $1 parking fee in the summer, a crowded time and not one we particularly recommend, because when you walk from the parking lot out on to the beach and turn to your right, in summer months this beach is a favorite picnicking and swimming spot. However, 100 yards past the life guard you escape the bulk of the crowd. As you move around the curve of the beach you have the choice of keeping to the edge of the water, or following the jeep tracks into the interior of this spit. You may be confused because Orient Point looks to the northeast, but this narrow strip of land that is Orient beach, four miles long, runs to the southwest.

What makes it unusual? It affords beautiful views of Gardiner's Bay and Shelter Island Sound. Wander at will amongst the scrub pine for you are never far from salt water on either side. There are two ponds in the interior which attract waterbirds, and here among the stunted pines and wetlands there is a herd of deer which comes and goes to the mainland and which, although we have seen their tracks many times, we have actually seen only fleetingly in winter. You cannot be quiet enough to surprise these wily, graceful creatures, but how they can conceal themselves in this narrow quarter is a mystery. They blend in and get lost as nature intended.

A good plan is to go out by the beach, pebbly but not bad footing, and back through the interior. If you get as far as the tip you will come to an old foundation of the

ORIENT BEACH STATE PARK

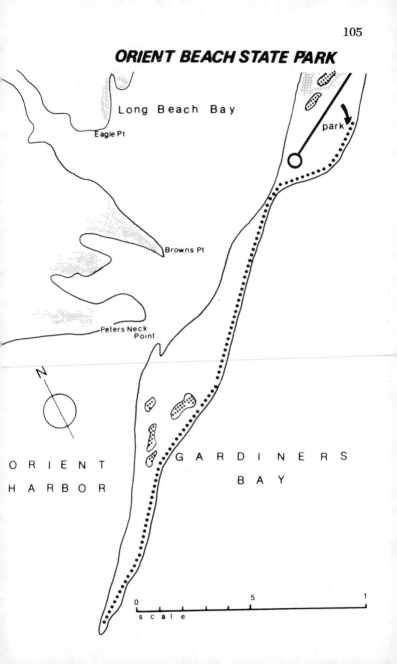

Long Beach Bay

Eagle Pt

park

Browns Pt

Peters Neck
Point

N

ORIENT

HARBOR

G A R D I N E R S

B A Y

0   .5   1

s c a l e

Orient light, which guided fishing boats into Greenport.

The place is out of this world. On a February 6th when we walked out to the point, the sky was clear and the Apollo 14 mission had landed on the moon. The refreshment building was boarded up and the ground was frozen. The sun was low, the moon stood out clearly in the dark afternoon sky, and the question arose: What is there in the nature of man that compels him to walk a lonely beach, to spy on wild creatures, to search to find the undisturbed places beyond?

37. Cedar Beach Point

The southwest tip of Great Hog Neck is a low lying, beautifully arched beach and salt meadow set aside as Cedar Beach Point County Preserve. It is remote, a good distance east on the north fork, and well off the arteries of main highways. Great Hog Neck is an odd shaped peninsula between Little Peconic Bay and Shelter Island Sound, with its devotees and many fine summer homes.

Cedar Beach Point is no dramatic sweep of sand, it does have a quality and spirit all its own, however, so that we have found ourselves walking here again and again along the edges of the Bay. The large parking lot requires a Southold permit and is crowded in summer but our walks here have been limited to the other times of year when we never encounter more than a car or two.

The way to get here is not direct. You turn south off Route 24 after leaving Peconic, headed east, on the first road right, South Harbor Road, then left and follow around south again on Bay View Road till it curves at the point. The parking lot is at the place where the beach curves westward to an inlet about a mile beyond, so follow along here by the water's edge and come back on the sandy upper beach. It's a beach of shells, unusual on Long Island which is not noted for the variety of shells. But of those few species which abound there is a tremendous range of shape and color. Millions of baby's cradles or boatshells heaped upon each other in windrows form the tideline. There are jingle shells like translucent flower petals in their array of yellow and orange, to ivory and eggshell colors. One day we collected twelve sizes of the delicate, fluted scallop shell in an equal number of colors. Then, at low tide, the marshy areas are dotted with the channelled and knobbed whelks that the seagulls bring to feast upon. These are the little monsters whose rasplike tongues can suck a helpless clam from his shell and devour him. On a clear day it seems you can reach out and touch Jessup's Neck, which pokes out from the opposite shore, and Shelter Island blends into the background

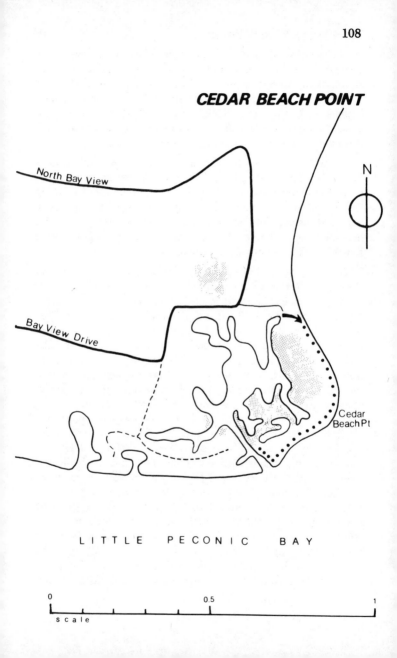

CEDAR BEACH POINT

North Bay View

N

Bay View Drive

Cedar Beach Pt

LITTLE PECONIC BAY

0   0.5   1
scale

to become part of the mainland. There is considerable boat traffic too, a variety of working and pleasure craft to attract your attention. The salt marsh to the back with the tide of clear waters rushing in and out through the narrow inlet is fascinating, and you can continue right to sit behind a lovely dune, sheltered, and catching the sun all day, eventually retracing your footsteps. But you'll tarry because of the bird activity in the marsh, certainly the greater yellowlegs bobbing in the shallows as is their strange habit.

Because the elevation of land is not ever far above the sea and there is so much cleared farmland at the east end of Long Island, the sky is a real eminence out here. You realize how little you see of it in a city. The sky plays a vital part in setting the mood of each day, influences the aspect of the beach, subtly puts its mark on sand and sea. By special emphasis it seems more brooding, more joyous, more mysterious out here. Sunsets are special—and another reason to lure you to return.

38. Morton National Wildlife Refuge

Dividing Little Peconic Bay and Noyack Bay, jutting out from the north shore of the south fork of the Island, just above Watermill, is Jessup's Neck. Of the numerous points, necks and promontories that jut into the waters surrounding Long Island, this offers wide variety of terrains, and walking here is great for many reasons. It is the Elizabeth Alexandra Morton Wild Life Refuge, and is managed by the US Government Fish and Wildlife Service. There is a devoted naturalist tending the place. His office is in the little building to the right beyond the parking area, and he'll probably be able to answer any questions you have. Walking, you can spend an hour or a day, come back again and again, never tire of the combination of beach, pond, woods and wetlands here.

The refuge is 8 miles northeast off the Montauk Highway, Exit #8, in Southampton, and the way is well marked. Follow along toward North Sea, and you will drive into the grounds through a gate on the northern side of Noyac Road; park here near an old barn a few hundred yards beyond. Register in the little hut where there is a map and pictures.

The path down to the bay is about a half mile and planted with many kinds of berry bushes—delectables for the land birds who frequent this quiet sanctuary. There is honeysuckle, myrtle, and rural charm. Be quiet and alert. We have come down this path of an early evening and surprised a graceful doe feasting on these same bushes. The path emerges upon a long narrow strip of beach on the bay with a small inlet from the bay on the right. Birds are in the inlet, and now and then a clammer leans out of his boat to scoop the bottom with his clamming rake. There will be the occasional boating party pulled up on the beach to swim. In fall or winter you'll see scallop boats in the bay dragging, though these juicy morsels are dwindling alarmingly, and nowhere else in the world does such a tiny, sweet, tender scallop exist.

You walk directly north about a mile and a half and come to a sharp rise and spread of land on a wooded promontory.

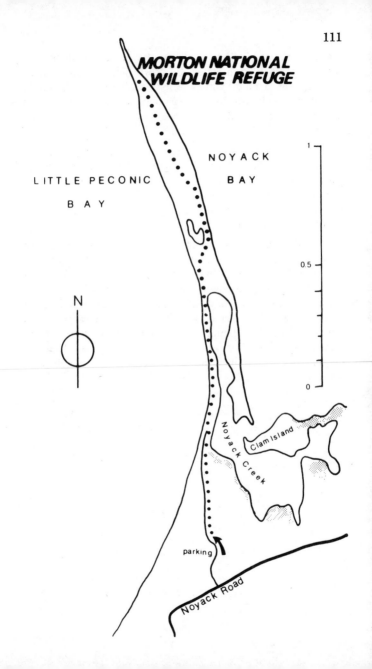

We like to walk in the woods on the path and all the way out to the point, then return by the beach, but altogether it then is over 6 miles and is a long walk. At the beginning of the wooded path there was once a farmhouse. In the spring a carpet of daffodils appears out of the myrtle, splendid in color in this secluded habitat.

In the spring woods, during the warbler migration you see some fifteen different varieties flitting among the big oaks before the leaves come on. And down on the beach near the pond to the west of the neck, look out to the weir where the osprey often sits on a pole where the pickings are concentrated for him.

The Morton Refuge can be a cool and refreshing place walking along the neck in summer, and in winter, when the bay freezes solid, if the winds across the ice are too chilling, there are many protected acres of woodland to the east before you reach the bay, and calm shelter for a walk under cover. One early spring we discovered a strangely eerie sight of dry white bones in a bed of greenest myrtle, the carcass of a deer dead of starvation or exhaustion. Later the ranger told us he had taken the skeleton to a school for preservation.

39. Horton Point

The Horton Point Lighthouse sits serenely, looking something like a canvas by Edward Hopper, high over the waters of Long Island Sound facing Connecticut. It is the chief ornament of a tree-shaded Town of Southold park, which is a beautiful place to picnic.

An extraordinarily long set of wooden steps takes you down to the boulder strewn beach. In all kinds of weather it is picturesque because of fisher-folk. They take blackfish from around those rocks. They dig their poles into the sand, light their pipes, and keep an eye on the floats, ready to jump and reel in when they bob. We always check to see if they have a few swimming about in their pails.

Walking on Horton's beach can be rough because of the pebbles, but good for massaging the insteps. Snorkelling is popular here. It's one of the few places on Long Island where we see people in wet suits with oxygen tanks and flippers. The huge rocks are relics of the ice age.

There is a long beach stretch here to the west that seems uninhabited, very wide with lots of driftwood. And the flotsam that heaves itself up on a beach is fascinating.

Standing on these north shore bluffs makes Long Island's formation in the geological past become fundamentally clear. You can imagine the great pushing blade of the glaciers, for geologists say Long Island is wholly the result of the glaciers, shoving a wide, wide swath of sand, soil, rock, tops of mountains southward like a massive dozer and piling it here. Then the ice melted and the waters ran off, washing the soils southward into a plain. And as they dropped to the ocean, the colossal scale of the whole thing can be appreciated when you realize that ocean was raised to its present level, over 300 ft. higher than it had been, by the melted ice to form the Long Island Sound. And what capriciousness there was in shoving and raising the level of the waters can be seen in the structure of peninsulas and spits and tiny islands which make up the shape of the map today.

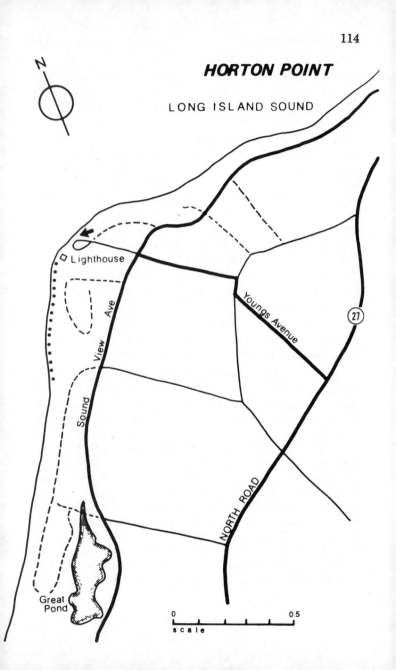

HORTON POINT

LONG ISLAND SOUND

N

Lighthouse

Sound View Ave

Youngs Avenue

27

NORTH ROAD

Great Pond

0   scale   0.5

And the force that could bring these huge boulders can be better appreciated when you walk along the beach here comparing your size to their size. Surely the experience is a universal one. One that will linger with you as long as you have your memory.

A word on getting here. Take the new four lane Route 27 east from Mattituck to the very end and continue on for another half mile on the road toward Greenport. Then north on Youngs Avenue, which bisects the highway, to the end of the road.

40. Wildwood State Park

Wildwood State Park is well out on the island, 73 miles east of New York City, has a frontage a little over three and a half miles on the Long Island Sound, is situated on high ground with high bluffs, and covers a little over 500 acres, a plot of ground shaped roughly rectangular. There is good walking along pebbly north shore beach here. Also, within the park, there are fire roads or jeep trails through woodland areas which cover a distance of almost 5 miles, all amply cleared trails, and easy walking straightaway and fairly level, nothing strenuous. So this is a place that is open, protected, quiet, wooded, with easy to follow dirt roads. And you can walk on them at a good clip.

Many of the north shore beaches are private, not allowing easy access without trespassing, but here is a large parking lot with a broad macadam walkway leading down a gradual slope, less than a half mile, to the beach. The sand doesn't shift along these north shore beaches rapidly as it does along the Atlantic. The water freezes up much more quickly and warms up earlier in the spring. The ground is gravelly and there are quite a few boulders, debris of the glacial period. Protected as the beach is by these high bluffs, it is a marked contrast to the ocean shore and offers good variety to a beach walker. There's less severe buffeting in windy weather, too. Those close relatives of the crab, barnacles, have attached themselves to all boulders, seaweed in many forms is exposed, periwinkles and whelks abound. The narrow strip of this tidal zone teams with life, hidden between rocks, and usually ignored by all except the most curious persons. Wildwood State Park, however, does have a considerable population because of a large tent camping area and also trailer camp, so it is a popular weekend retreat and no place to walk the beach during summer months if you seek a lonely stretch. Plan to walk in Wildwood out of season, when it will be rewarding.

To get to Wildwood take Route 54, Hulse Log Road, north from Route 25A. It is just east of Wading River.

WILDWOOD STATE PARK

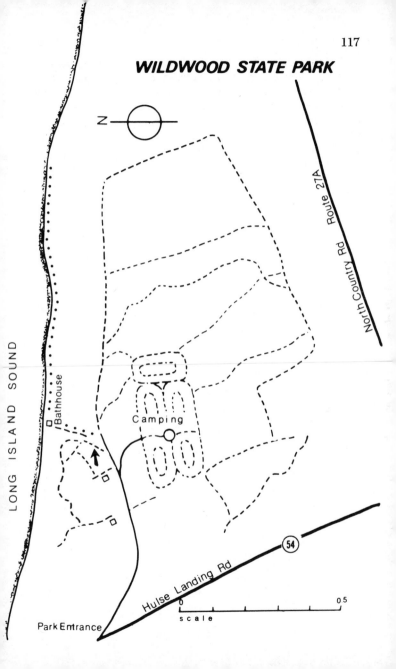

N

LONG ISLAND SOUND

Bathhouse

Camping

North Country Rd   Route 27A

Hulse Landing Rd

54

Park Entrance

0   5
scale

Quite naturally the inland trails are places less frequented, although they are more protected and easier walking. If it weren't for the trees along the north shore, erosion would have taken most of Long Island into the Sound. So walk here to discover the woodland, the home of numerous insects, birds and mammals, and bring along a curiosity to get to know still another tree, shrub or creature with whom we share the earth.

41. Roanoke Beach

The town of Riverhead maintains a beach at the end of Roanoke Avenue on Long Island Sound. The bluffs on the sound are extremely high, the beach at the tide line quite pebbly and, just west a half mile, strewn with two ship hulks, wrecks of some time past. It's a steep walk down to the beach from the parking spot. Turn left and walk a couple of hundred yards and you will be alone.

For miles along here the border of high wooded bluffs obscures any houses and there is a feeling of immense loneliness. There are especially wide areas, and big tangles of the purple beach pea, sea rocket and bishop's weed. Some reeds at the base of the bluffs are so tall you can be completely concealed by them. It is nice exploring territory. Tangles of growth conceal old driftwood, and there are wild beach flowers. Fishing offshore here must be pretty good, there are frequently clusters of small boats bobbing not far out, and an occasional surfcaster.

We have walked this beach at many seasons because its undeveloped qualities appeal to us. In a winter rain the Connecticut shoreline is completely obscured. With snow on the frozen ground you cover distances faster. In early spring we find trailing arbutus on paths up the bluffs, with wintergreen and partridge berry. The trailing arbutus is particularly satisfying to come upon in blossom, such a delicate fragrance, and tiny palest lavender petals. On fresh bright sunny weekends, the promise of a good breeze brings many sails out on the sound and the clarity lets you see details on the opposite shores. Falling autumn leaves pile up in the gullies, cover over paths and rustle when you pass along. Because we never have any particular objective in mind we always look at a watch as we start off headed west, and when we remember to look again we are always surprised by the lateness of the hour. We usually take along field glasses and a camera.

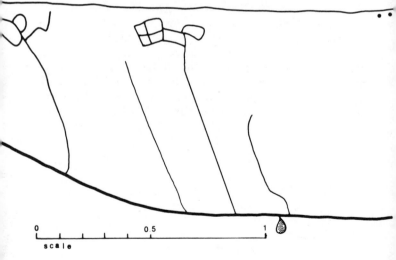

scale

How to get there? Follow Roanoke Avenue north until it ends at Sound Avenue. Then turn left, west, and go a short distance to the first road, Park Road. Turn right, north, and follow up and down a hill or two. The road stops in a parking area which overlooks Roanoke Beach.

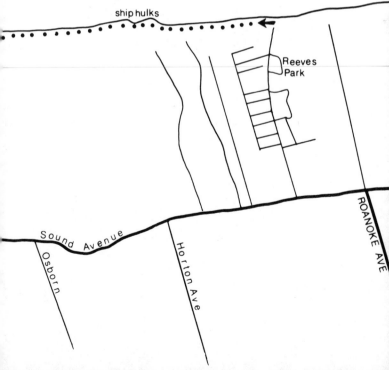

Notes

Notes

Notes

Notes

Notes

Notes

Notes

About the authors.

Priscilla and Rodney Albright are adopted New Yorkers. She spent her youth in Olean, New York, he in Indianapolis. But both came East to college and have lived in the metropolis, more or less, ever since. Priscilla has devoted her energies to social work. Rod has been producing television commercials for a large advertising agency in New York City. They took time away from the city to raise a family in Bedford Village, Westchester County, then moved back into the city in 1965 so they could walk to work.

Walking has been a particular pleasure of theirs for a long time. Wherever they are—Oregon or California, Indiana or Maine, Paris or Dubrovnik—they are apt to set out to explore the surrooundings by foot. Long Island is a special place for them. Stretching eastward from the city, the Albrights have crossed and crisscrossed it weekend after weekend.

They are members of The Audubon Society, The Nature Conservancy, The Wilderness Society, The New York/New Jersey Trail Conference, The National Geographic Society. All attesting to their love of the out-of-doors and a sensitivity to preserving America's natural heritage.

The Pequot Press

OLD CHESTER ROAD
CHESTER, CONNECTICUT 06412